Maryann,

HEAVEN
HELP ME

Donna Criqui

BALBOA PRESS
A DIVISION OF HAY HOUSE

I understand you have been through many challenges.

I feel your inner strength. Remember to go within... love you 1st... trust your inner compass. One step at a time... one day @ a time

Sending love,
Donna
xo

Cover and Author Photography: Bri Morse www.brimorsephotography
@brimorsephotography

Cover Graphics Art Credit:
Sam Smith M-D
Ssmddesign@icloud.com
@ssmddesign

Balboa Press books may be ordered through booksellers or by contacting:

Balboa Press
A Division of Hay House
1663 Liberty Drive
Bloomington, IN 47403
www.balboapress.com
1 (877) 407-4847

Because of the dynamic nature of the Internet, any web addresses or links contained in this book may have changed since publication and may no longer be valid. The views expressed in this work are solely those of the author and do not necessarily reflect the views of the publisher, and the publisher hereby disclaims any responsibility for them.

The author of this book does not dispense medical advice or prescribe the use of any technique as a form of treatment for physical, emotional, or medical problems without the advice of a physician, either directly or indirectly. The intent of the author is only to offer information of a general nature to help you in your quest for emotional and spiritual well-being. In the event you use any of the information in this book for yourself, which is your constitutional right, the author and the publisher assume no responsibility for your actions.

Any people depicted in stock imagery provided by Getty Images are models, and such images are being used for illustrative purposes only.
Certain stock imagery © Getty Images.

Print information available on the last page.

ISBN: 978-1-9822-1559-0 (sc)
ISBN: 978-1-9822-1561-3 (hc)
ISBN: 978-1-9822-1560-6 (e)

Library of Congress Control Number: 2018913148

Balboa Press rev. date: 01/08/2019

CONTENTS

ACKNOWLEDGMENT

I wish to thank first and foremost our loving Creator who has spent this lifetime showing me the truth in the most gorgeous ways. His power, love and support are available always. I love you and give you my purpose and direction so that I may be a warrior on your behalf. Thank you for your trust. I hope I serve you well.

I also would like to thank my beautiful inspirations and the reason for giving this life my all, my daughters Morgan and Jadin. You have been with me during so many miracles and signs. You yourselves have pointed out the deeper messages and signs to ME. I have learned through you and because of you. You have always believed I could, even when I didn't see a way. I pushed forward with God for you and found out I could.

I acknowledge my Mom and Dad for the providing me the foundation of God, love, family and faith. You were a shining example of how to be in the world with generosity, compassion, strength, empathy and joy. Thank you for your love that expands beyond this life and your continued presence daily and in my heart.

I wish to thank Eric for believing in my dream of helping others on a larger scale. You spoke only goodness over my vision - even when it meant me sitting quietly for hours on end. Thank you especially for listening to me process and your shared love of God.

And to acknowledge especially my wonderfully wise teachers who walked the talk always, Nancy Serak (Ariel), Carol Parsons, and Louise Laffey. You all have been patient through my questioning and repeating of old ways. You each helped me to reach for better in your different wisdom, teaching and leading. I am grateful for your presence and role in my life.

And to all of the beautiful people on this planet who spread the Light, inspire, reach and grow to make this planet more loving and awake. Keep going, your love makes a difference. If this is new to you, please acknowledge yourself for even beginning your search. Thank you for taking a step and enjoy your awakening path unfolding.

PREFACE

Hello friends and welcome! About 10 years ago I was told by my angels I would be writing a book with the title, "HEAVEN HELP ME." The content of this book has expanded from my initial thinking. I had been receiving undeniable heavenly support during an extremely difficult time of my life. I was told by the angels to wait in writing the book when I thought it was time. They said to me, "you have more to share that you haven't experienced yet." They were 100% correct.

I will take you through my actual life experiences of how God can present himself to us in our environment and how to recognize Divine help for yourself in your daily life. I will give examples how to be in flow with creation and attract miracles, and how to create a closer relationship with our invisible support system that is available to us all. I will also address the concept of how we are all energy and how our personal energy has a direct effect on the life we experience. Recently I kept feeling an inner prompting it's time, write it now. Once I began, it poured through me like a full flow of water through an open faucet.

I hope to help people who feel separate or passed over at times to understand how the Universe supports and responds to us always and how much we are loved. That we all receive messages often but we ourselves are overlooking them. By the end you will see what a connected and aware life can look like and maybe have some fun with getting signs, answers, and guidance for yourself.

I wish to help you learn how to create a life that feels amazing by you being the manager and director of your mind/energy. And I will address by the end the importance to have a love and respect for yourself as a foundation to create a world that feels more pleasing. I love to see the excitement when my friends and clients come back to me with their own stories of a sign or seemingly miraculous events that unfolded for them since our last conversation.

When my friends or clients come to me for help with something troubling them, I ask them questions such as….. well did you ask the Universe for guidance? Or did you ask for clarity around what's happening, or have you asked that the best answer comes clearly and it brings you peace? Or ask about your next right step? My favorite is well, have your surrendered it completely? The overwhelming response is, well…..no I didn't. This is a two way interactive street my friends, we can open the communication and receive answers from the Universe more quickly and easier than you think!

We tend to complain (which is us just being human) and forget we can seek the best solutions in our heavenly support. And so many of us have felt as if we are a victim of life in a series of random circumstances. There are messages for us to observe that come to us every day. My goal in writing this book is to raise your awareness in how you can develop a personal relationship with your beautiful invisible lifeline that is with you 24/7. Know it all begins with YOU. I wish to help empower you if you so desire to make your life easier and more fun. I will provide you concepts and tools to get you through your day, your week and your life.

The chapters on Universal Energy and Advanced Universal Energy I wrote to share with you what a developed spiritual relationship can look like. Things happened that surprised me beyond what I was ever taught in my reiki classes. I learned to observe what I saw with a curiosity and trust more deeply. There is so much more available to us from the invisible plane than I was ever taught as a child. I am not special and I was a big skeptic at one time. I too doubted that I could ever experience the relationship and understanding that I now have. You can do this, this invisible world is available to support us all. The only thing in your way is your own beliefs.

The beginning of this book will take you initially through my spiritual evolution and how I came to understand a bit more about the world we can't see. My story begins with what I was taught as a young girl. Being taught about fear and limitations, shame and sin. Clearly being told don't question the teachings…..just do and think as I tell you. I will share with you some the strange experiences of how I was led to becoming more aligned with God's love, beauty and grace and ultimately a spiritual teacher and intuitive energy healer.

My hope is that this book will not only be entertaining, but perhaps help you understand the possibilities available to you knowing you can easily put this into practice for yourself. Ideas that stretch beyond the ordinary way of navigating life. At one time I was told anything outside of my strictly religious teachings were a wrong and forbidden path and only special chosen people hear God.

If this is a new concept for you, I hope my stories and teachings I have learned over 20 plus years may serve as a way for you to recognize ways that our invisible support system is reaching out to YOU. How it helps you to be in alignment and one with God. To remember to ask questions or ask for help and invite God's communication and intervention. Nothing is ever too trivial or too big for Divine assistance. Understand we all have times where it appears nothing is happening. But trust that the Universe is working in ways we don't always understand with a higher wisdom on our behalf.

In all of my stories there are underlying lessons and teachings. Every outcome has shown me that God is love, that we are cared for with a much higher wisdom than ours alone. I know we all hear not to worry, there is a perfect design of a bigger plan. I have learned that things unfold with grace more often than not when we get out of our own way and we make room for God. Invite Him in and allow Him to work through our lives. Everything the Universe provides for us on our path is unfolding perfectly, even what we perceive as negative.

Who better for us to trust than the Higher Wisdom of our loving Source who created the entire Universe, where planets don't collide, and the earth revolves around the sun every day flawlessly as it's intended. Knowing that this same Source that is keeping everything in the Universe running as it has from the beginning of creation is available to us in every moment and has a higher plan than our limited understandings. Pretty amazing realization for me thing for me. Why would I ever doubt?

I had some scary and odd happenings at 4 years old that no one I knew could provide an explanation. I became aware early on that grownups didn't know everything. Which sent me on a lifelong journey of seeking answers. In essence, there is a much nicer way to go through life than my early teachings. To know that we are all loved, we are all worthy of receiving miracles and that Heaven is always around us, within us, and accessible to us. No degree or specialness needed.

Within each chapter I will chime in with a bit of my evolved perspective explaining more of what my 20 plus years as a spiritual student and teacher has taught me.

My intro is about a very close friend and client who wishes to remain anonymous. Names in her story have been changed for her protection. But I feel it demonstrates an emotion we all feel at times. I am sure you can relate to those times where you have felt a degree of desperation, where you feel totally lost and alone. You wonder where is God, how could He let this happen to you? I love how my friend shares how she changed her approach in the way she prayed for help after hearing nothing during the most difficult time of her life.

The Intro may seem off track, but stick with me. The rest of the book is a bit more light hearted. But I wanted to explore a human experience that we all share in some way or another. Those moments that we really could use a lifeline of help. Where it feels like an emergency of great magnitude on a deep soul level. As if the world had no idea the amount of pain you endured in a situation and you felt there was no solution.

My friend who you are about to meet in my intro has been through quite a bit. At one point, there was a time where she prayed as if her wellbeing and life depended on it. She learned to really lean on her inner wisdom and connection more deeply than ever when she was leaving an extremely verbally and emotionally and occasionally physically abusive relationship. She didn't know where to turn.

She had a few key friends who loved her, but no one could take the steps for her that she herself needed to take. She learned to change *what* she was asking for or *ask in a different way*. When she changed her daily focus and self-talk, doors opened in amazingly new ways.

I myself through the years have evolved in my sense of self, my view of my *deserving* God's help. Asking myself always what is *my role* and responsibility in creating my life and what is showing up for me? I invite you to have fun recognizing the abundance of help in your own life and the divine hand at play. To look for the little synchronicities along the way to help lead, inspire and comfort you. I invite you to start looking around you every day observing Heaven helping you in so many ways, it all begins with YOU!

Introduction

It seemed Sherry had not enough money to take care of herself and her three young children. She felt so alone in her pain with no direction of how to even begin this process. She managed to leave a living hell, starting fresh with the freedom to live peacefully and safely by her rules and in a loving household. Not saying this process wasn't terrifying, but once she recognized Heaven was helping her she had the courage to take the leap. For a while it seemed Heaven didn't hear her at all.

Sherry was in a very verbally, emotionally and on occasion physically abusive relationship for years. It didn't start out abusive, but the last 5 years were not good. She felt so stuck and felt as if her spirit inside was dying bit by bit with each passing day. This was not even close to how she dreamt her ideal family would look.

Sherry was told by her fiancé Keith who was her partner for 12 years and the father of her three children that he acted the way he did towards her because of her. She was the problem. She was a strong girl, so she thought. Sherry loved being a mom, had lots of friends and loved her job. Looking from the outside, it appeared as if she had a great life.

Sherry deep down wondered what was she doing wrong? She knew her fiancé was acting like an ass but wondered what was her responsibility in what was happening. It added to her confusion when she finally confided in a woman hoping for guidance who said, well no one is innocent! You HAD to do something. This was the advice from a Christian woman in good standing with her church and counseled couples. Looking back Sherry sees that was really wrong information.

One day Sherry came across some information that rang through her to her core. She didn't know how bad things had gotten until one day when she had to use to the ladies room at a city hospital while visiting her dad. She stumbled upon a really big poster on the back of the stall.

Yep, there she was right there in the ladies room when it hit her like a ton of bricks. There are actually entire organizations designed for the purpose to rescue women from her experience. Her jaw dropped... she read the bold print with a helpline phone number and the following.…..
Are you bullied, manipulated, called names, controlled, talked down to, intimidated, physically restrained against your will, hit, and the list went on and on.

She counted, there were about 13 signs of abuse on that poster, she experienced 11. Sherry silently thought OMG, I am an abused woman? How did it get this bad? She felt maybe she exaggerated, but in looking back she now knows she was being brainwashed in Keith's words, "this is what happens in a normal relationship."

In the past he mocked her for even thinking that he was abusing her. She said to me, well I never had a broken bone or a black eye.

It happened slowly over the years. Sherry was spoken to with degrading words saying she is pathetic, or being called a joke or names mocking her. She often experienced manipulation, being talked down to or being harassed for seemingly everything - even just being her well-meaning self.

Sherry felt like she was in a relationship with Dr. Jekyll and Mr. Hyde. One minute a very nice person, Keith was very charming when there were people around. But when the doors closed or people left, he turned into a completely different person. Before seeing the poster in the hospital around abuse, Sherry questioned herself wondering if Keith's actions could be her fault.

Their relationship wasn't always like it evolved into. Sherry and her partner had some workable issues for years. They went through a good time for a while. Their happiest time was right before he changed for the worst. A very dark side seemed to surface like a flip switched. It started out with the way he talked to her and would treat her, but the abuse got progressively worse until one day a neighbor witnessed her being chased to her car.

Sherry's goal in being a mom at this stage was to give her children the best and most loving experience for their childhood. She tried to protect her little loves the best she could from what they saw at home by getting them all away from the house every single day.

When it was just Sherry and the kids they were free to just love each other, play and have fun unencumbered.

Sherry and her three children would spend all day with friends, museums, pools, rock climbing walls, roller skating, bowling and enjoying the sunshine and nature by going parks in every reach of them and the surrounding counties. They began to leave home all day whenever they knew Keith was going to be home. It felt as if the walls were closing in and the torment was 24/7.

Sherry knew what her kids were being exposed was not good as a foundation for a child. Witnessing the way their mom was being treated as their normal? She was concerned her kids would repeat what was being modeled as a relationship in their own adult experiences someday.

Keith would always sabotage their fun and there was always drama. Sherry also realized life was much happier and easier without him home when he traveled to Chicago one week. How peaceful and lighthearted their week was in their home, singing, giggling freely together. They were all so very relaxed and happy. Sherry noticed a difference in her kids behavior with just them, totally love and joy. She started get more clarity and perspective about her situation.

When Keith returned from his trip, so did the pit in her stomach. Sherry said to herself one day, this is not who I am. I am not angry and hostile by nature at ALL. She didn't want to play in Keith's world anymore defending herself, protecting herself. Getting attacked from the time she woke up until bed? Sherry yearned for a home filled with fun, love and joy for herself and for her children like they had when they were alone. She dreamt for this be their everyday life. Not what they were seeing and experiencing watching in their world presently.

One day Sherry heard guidance as Keith had her pinned against her dresser, twisting and hurting her arm. Sherry began to fight back trying to break free and was getting ready to give Keith a piece of her mind. Sherry took a deep breath to tell him off and she looked in his eyes, he had an evil look. He wasn't even in his eyes anymore, she didn't recognize the man looking back at her in the moment. A shot of terror ran through her body leaving a sinking feeling. She heard something deep inside say clearly and very urgently....*walk away, he is going to kill you.* Sherry got away without a word, got the kids in the car and left to let things calm down.

Sherry kept begging … Heaven help me, heaven help me!! Where are you? Please rescue me!! Send me someone who will take us away and protect us. Why aren't you helping me? Don't my children and I matter to you? What do I have to do? How could you let this happen to us?

Sherry prayed many times a day for help. However, around this topic she did not seem to be getting any guidance. Being stuck was all Sherry could seem to think about. Until one day Sherry began to pray, what do I need to do God? Why am I not hearing you? I know you are always with me and the truth is you are always here. Why the silence? What do you want me to know?

Sherry in her silent reflection felt like she was beginning to receive some higher wisdom. She began to learn how to ask questions and work with God with a slight difference than she had been. By working, I mean how to ask the right questions, and how to understand guidance and answers. Being aware. And with getting clear on the next right step, she learned it's up to us to take action. As opposed to what she had been doing which was begging and pleading, asking to be rescued from her situation. Sherry felt from her reflection that SHE needed to take the steps, God would be with her but she needed to get strong and make the changes within.

Sherry began to gain more in confidence and understanding her inner voice. Sherry no longer prayed as if she was forgotten. Instead she began to ask God, "show me how we can leave, how can I afford to provide for my children alone and please help me to have the courage do this." No longer asking to be rescued.

She also began asking questions that would bring her the peace she needed to move forward such as; "is it me?" and "Can you please let me know you are here?" Sherry began to recognize and trust in her connection with the Divine. She had the conviction and courage to proceed to a better life. Realizing now *she* needed to make the steps, but she didn't have to do alone.

Sherry felt she was finally heard by changing her prayers asking to be aligned with her truth. Which led to her changing her perspective in her own mind from being a victim to becoming stronger and determined. Sherry recognized she and her children had the right to a safe and happy home and that the actions towards her were not acceptable ever!

And her biggest motivator in leaving was that her children were watching. She knew she was their example of what to accept and who to be as a woman, and how to treat a woman.

Enough of the yuk right? But I wanted to let you know how important it was for me to deepen my trust in the Universe with witnessing and living stories such as Sherry's and one of the reasons I titled this book, "Heaven Help Me." We all share stories such as this in one way or another where we don't know where to turn. This is when most people reach out to me as a healer, as an energy coach and friend. This where our faith, self love and our awareness come into play. I don't know what I would do without my faith. When life gets challenging I lean into God with all I have. And it is also so much fun when I see God's little "atta girl" in the spaces.

I am glad I listened to the angels 10 years ago in waiting to write this book. I feel I have more to offer in not only how to interpret and feel Heaven's help in countless ways. Such as understanding how we set things in motion and how we play a role in what turns up for us. It has everything to do with our focus, our minds, thoughts and energy vibration that we hold which plays a huge part in our experiences. WE ARE ENERGY! Life is simply a mirror showing us the energy we hold inside of us which is being reflected in our life experiences.

When Sherry stopped thinking she was stuck and she instead replaced her focus to more empowering thoughts, words and prayers….things began to change.

Instead she prayed, "show me how to leave," turning to God for strength and direction. That's exactly what began to show up for her.

I have quite a fun story around how Sherry found out it wasn't her doing something wrong as a person in her abusive experience in the Chapter titled, The Road to Better. She felt so supported as her questions were clearly being answered. She did come to the realization one day that maybe God wanted her to grow and understand how strong she is, and maybe God wants her to rescue herself. Sherry had to get stronger, SHE had to decide her worth. But she didn't have to walk this journey alone. She wasn't shown the whole plan ahead of time, just feeling strongly to take that first step and then the next one. We all have heard the famous quote by Martin Luther King, Jr that I have learned is 100% truth.

> *"Take the first step in faith. You don't have to see the whole staircase, just take the first step." ~ Martin Luther King Jr.*

Sherry also understands in hindsight where she was stuck, her mind was dwelling on the impossible. When we are focused around fearful thoughts, it is not believing that God is always with us or trusting that He is working on our behalf. We may feel this way because life doesn't feel great during challenging times. We often assume God's absence in our difficult moments. We often are not patient, worry, obsess and want results now. **Fear is the *opposite* of faith.** That is putting our agenda in charge instead of the highest Wisdom available to us. Fear means WE have just stepped out of alignment with God and how we are perceiving things. It's a quick fix truly, just choose to step back into alignment in our thoughts and feel into the peace of oneness with God.

Have you ever heard "where your attention goes, energy flows?" For Sherry having thoughts such as there's no way out, I am hopelessly stuck were her all-consuming thoughts all day long trying to figure out how to leave. So there she was, stuck and unhappy. Not realizing she was affirming "she was all alone, no one understands, there's no way out," were her thoughts all day everyday. It was absolutely true! UNTIL SHE SWITCHED HER FOCUS!

Where your mind dwells really is like a prayer. If your mind dwells on what you don't want, you get more of what you don't want. Where ever your attention is focused the energy expands and brings you where you place your attention.

Sherry also began to visualize before bed a happy peaceful time with her children, laughing, playing in an open field basking in the sunshine feeling free! Instead of focusing on being stuck and unhappy, Sherry instead began to ask, "what's the direction I needed to take to assure we would be ok financially and safe, and peaceful." "What's my next step, please if I am not hearing you tell me again. Thank you God!"

Please understand in this book, I may refer to God, Jesus, Holy Spirit, Universe, Mary, angels, or Source. Daily I even address my angels when I have a question, "Hey Guys can you please show me where I left my keys?" 99% of the time my eyes are taken immediately to them before I am done even asking, drawn like a magnet to their location. However you address your source, I honor. If you prefer God, Jesus, Source, Universe, Buddha, Quan Yin, Ganesh etc...... it is yours how you address your Higher Power. I honor your beliefs. Thanks for honoring mine.

I believe there is more than one way to find God. Many paths to the same destination. Many religions, many perceptions. What works for you is *your* personal truth. What resonates and supports you is your own personal journey. If I can offer anything that speaks to your truth, or maybe open your mind to new ideas of how to enhance your life then awesome! If something doesn't speak to you just leave it on the page.

Have you ever not been sure as to how to ask for help or wonder why you are not getting answers to your prayers? How do we create better in our lives? What's the best way to handle experiences that arise we perceive could hurt us in some way? How can we shift our moods, mind and experiences? How do we let go of negative energy? I have learned situations can shift quickly and I will share tools with you I picked up through the years. Heaven helps us constantly, but we also can help ourselves by being in trust, surrender, and how we focus our mind. And also our relationship within ourselves, and our beliefs.

If this idea of energy is new to you, maybe this explanation can help. Imagine that your own personal energy vibration as always broadcasting your personal kind of radio broadcast. Wherever you are mostly in your thoughts, moods, your focus, your words, feelings, beliefs, your life experiences all play a role in your energy vibration. This energy travels from you like a signal from a radio tower out to the universe. And the Universe acts like a receiver.

The Universe receives the messages you are broadcasting 24/7. The Universe says.....got it! This is what you are asking for....and returns back to you more of the vibe that you are sending out. (Are you sending lots of love and joy, therefore get more love and joy, or do you send lots of worry or complaints? Therefore getting more to worry or complain about!)

When you consciously manage your thoughts, your beliefs, and have a healthy self love, and are aware and present with your Universal connection, you in essence are managing your energy. Which is what is being vibrated out to the Universe and is returned back to us like a boomerang.

I have always understood God has all the power and the answers. But I now see so much begins with me, how I affect my life with my energy and core beliefs consciously or unconsciously. My approach to life and how to navigate is now faster and easier to bring peace and see results quickly. Life is better when we live LOVE based and in alignment with the Source of all creation. But my friends it all begins with you.

I hope you enjoy reading the stories of my evolution and discoveries along the way that you can give a try for yourself. My wish is for you to know that you are worthy, you are able, and you are treasured beyond measure and very loved. May magic and miracles unfold before you! Much love, Donna xo

CHAPTER 1

The Questioning Began Early!

I have had some really odd experiences since I was a little girl. I came to understand quickly the invisible topic was taboo. No one else in my world around me at the time experienced anything like I was experiencing. Like seeing the Blessed Mother around 4 years old in my bedroom or feeling someone there during the middle of the night when I couldn't see anyone with the glow from my nightlight. I was hearing voices when no one was there. I was repeatedly tapped on the shoulder one night with a woman's voice whispering in my right ear, calling my name from the darkness. I would run into my mom and dad's room for help, only to be told by my mom to go back to bed it's your imagination.

My mom didn't believe me. How could she turn me back over to the invisible happenings in my room? I literally didn't sleep soundly until I was 28 years old. Because of my upbringing I was sure I did something wrong by experiencing the invisible, or thought it was the devil lurking.

I began Catholic School in first grade. We had religion class daily just as you would English or math class. The last thing I knew I was watching Sesame Street and Batman in the comfort of my living room.... laughing, having fun playing in my own little cozy world. The next thing I knew I was in boot camp for kiddies being told I am a sinner and would be punished and judged for all my wrongdoings someday.

Welcome to your new world!

My first grade nun Sister Aloysius introduced us to "Mr. Pointy" on our first day of school. Mr. Pointy was a paddle that was used for bad behavior. Yep, I was horrified! Where in the world did my parents send me? I watched many a kid unfairly accused and not guilty feel the sting at the end of that paddle. Sometimes a swat came for a typical kid thing like talking when you weren't supposed to, and sometimes without any proof - only Sister's assumption of guilt.

One day sister said to me, "Donna, surely you must have done something wrong I didn't see." (I knew where she was going with this.) Sister expressed to me she didn't remember me being hit with Mr. Pointy. I looked sister square in the eye and did something I felt so ashamed and knew it was wrong but what should I do? Fear won! In that split second of wrestling with choices, I told her, "Oh no sister, you DID hit me, don't you remember?" She didn't remember and I gave an Oscar winning performance! Sister believed me. (Hurray!) I escaped all year without a feeling the sting of that paddle. That to me was prize enough, I didn't need an Oscar!

Surely God was going to get me someday for lying to a nun. I pictured myself in heaven on trial one day with God, angrily throwing "the book" at me and shaking his finger in my face. In my mind the book was the bible being whirled at me by God and hitting my head. Who by the way I pictured as a man with a long glowing white beard in a robe who was not happy with me.

Holy Mary Mother of God

On a positive note, one thing that I really enjoyed religiously was the feeling I got when we prayed the rosary. Looking at the huge beautiful Blessed Mother statue on our playground, we gathered as a school and prayed a decade of the rosary in unison (10 Hail Mary's.) Afterwards we would sing one of the songs we would in church when we completed our prayers.

I know it sounds corny for such a young kid to appreciate those moments. There was something that was so wonderfully peaceful to me, reciting the prayers in the breeze and the sunshine - I loved Mary and wasn't sure why. Mary was Jesus's mother, what a special woman to God that He entrusted His only Son. Mysterious she was, I had questions and wanted to know more. I think another reason I enjoyed the connection to Mary was I felt she was not going to hurt me, judge me or see me as bad. Where I was told God would judge me and had the power to send me to hell.

Later in life I grew to go to Mary in prayer, for guidance and help. I appreciated the fact that Mary actually lived as a woman and a mother. I believe she even helped me with conception. My mom gave me a special prayer book that was given to her by my grandmother, the pages were very tattered from years of her heavy use. I was experiencing challenges in getting pregnant so I prayed to the Blessed Mother to help me conceive a sibling for my daughter Morgan. In the chapter Ask and it is Given, I share with you my moment which goes down as one of my lifetimes most special experiences and miracles that led to one of greatest treasures. Her name is Jadin Mary, my youngest daughter.

So taking this story back to my early school days, after we said the Rosary one day we received a gift when we got back to class.

The Glowing Gift

We were all in class about 3rd grade or so given these whitish/light green rosaries after recess and rosary time was over. I was so excited to have another rosary. I had gotten one for my first Holy Communion which was pure white, a had gorgeous multi-faceted crystal one, and I also had a pretty light blue one. Yep, my rosary collection was growing. Most kids collect baseball cards, my rosary collection was on point!

So in religion class that day we talked about how the devil would try to tempt Jesus. Sister told us with the enthusiasm of a great a story teller how the devil would try to come after us and throw us into temptation and he could be lurking invisibly around us! Well Holy Crap!! We may as well just watch a little Freddie Krueger in Nightmare on Elm Street while we are at it.

On this particular day, I left feeling uneasy on the bus ride going home and was on the lookout for the devil lurking around me. Was he on the bus with me? I was greatly relieved to be home with my mom and dad. I had dinner with my large family which comforted me. I so enjoyed the lively conversation with my older brothers and sisters. I looked up to them so much! Finally with the routine of my evening I completely forgot about what we talked about at school. I spent time with everyone, did the family thing and then I went to sleep. I hung my new rosary on the my dresser mirror which was across the room from my bed.

I woke up while everyone was still up watching TV in the next room. Then out of the quiet of the night, I screamed bloody murder. My parents came running in to see what I was freaking out about. I saw the rosary just hovering off of the floor and it was glowing brightly out of the darkness. It was activated and floating! The devil surely was pissed and in my room because of my love of God. It's happening, the devil was there to get me.

My mom burst into my room and turned on my light. My rosary was in place where I left it on my dresser. Turns out it was a glow in the dark rosary which nobody mentioned to me at school as they handed them out. I was relieved when my mom removed the rosary from my mirror and took with her.

Can you see where I may have gotten some messages that were fear based? I heard God was love, you can go to Him with anything, He will protect you. However, you have to earn it was also a message I was taught. Totally conditional and contradictory of love. And don't forget to live in fear! I would be judged upon my death for all the wrong I did and can only hope to get to heaven. I felt like a bolt of lightning would strike me at any given moment if God was angry with me. I am an 8 year old sinner.

My mom even said to my 40 something self when we lost my dog Lucky who was 16 years old, "See, if you would have gone to church this wouldn't have happened." Pausing and quietly smiling to myself, I said really mom, are you saying if I went to church my dog wouldn't have died?" Ever?? God bless my mom, it's her belief system and habits of throwing a bit of guilt to try to make a point. I mean she was born in the 1920's, totally different era and that was just the norm.

Even through all the erroneous teachings in my mind, all the rules, my greatest spiritual teacher was my mom. She was a good Catholic, an impeccable rule follower. Mom always did the right thing morally, especially regarding church doctrine. But as I approached my teens mom revealed a softer side to all of these beliefs. I soon began to feel it was ok to start to have my own feelings and conclusions around this strict church doctrine. Something began stirring deeper that allowed my broader thinking. If my mom contoured the beliefs to something more in alignment with LOVE, maybe it's ok to explore other people's perceptions about God.

Little Flower Pearls of Wisdom

My mom went to an all-girls Catholic High School, called the Little Flower in Philadelphia, Pennsylvania back in the 1940's. She spoke of her time there with such joy, as one of the best times in her life. She LOVED the order of nuns who taught her. My mom was an accomplished concert violinist and would go on trips with the girls orchestra lead by this order of Godly women. My mom in her day was written about in the Philadelphia paper as being the youngest Concert Meister in Philadelphia history. She was an amazingly gifted musician.

The nuns who were in charge of the Orchestra sounded like a lot fun, very loving and progressive for the 1940's. They would speak to the young girls with care, kindness and with humor. These ladies were respected, inspiring, open hearted leaders and role models to these young women.

The Sister's discussed the topic of baptism. They told the students that they believed God would let little babies into heaven even if they weren't baptized. If you are not Catholic, let me catch you up to the teachings from years ago. I was taught you must be baptized or would spend eternity in limbo. If you missed that boat, you were going to stay separate from God.

Never experiencing the bliss and reward of Heaven. That thought never seemed fair or right in my mind.

These wise ladies shared some deviation from the teachings I was taught. More in alignment with love.

Another of the teachings that never seemed not to fly with me was you must be Christian to get into Heaven. That in my mind this didn't sound like a loving God who made us all in His image. As a little girl I even began to question.....God who created each and every one of us, who decided who were our parents were going to be, all being born into certain countries and locations globally who were brought up to believe whatever the religion our parents believed or even no religion - these people would be punished for not believing as I was taught?

The Little Flower nuns told my mom that they believed people could get into heaven regardless of religious beliefs. Now THAT God to me was a loving God. And much more aligned with the idea that God loves *all* of His children. I started to have *more* questions, and was excited at the thought that there are more possibilities. When I did question the teachings at school as a young child, people got angry, lol. I would just walk away because it was easier.

Rhythm is gonna get ya, rhythm is gonna get ya tonight!

Thanks Gloria Estefan for this song playing in my mind while proofing this paragraph and me dancing at 6 a.m. to your memorable song! As I approached my teen years, my mom sat me down for "the talk."

A part of our talk about sex of course was about morality in waiting until marriage, then the progression of the talk led to the embarrassing chat around birth control.

As strict Catholic who was a true rule follower, my mom told me that Catholics don't believe in taking birth control but practiced the "rhythm method" instead. Meaning back in a certain era you counted about 14 days to know the perceived fertile time of your cycle. The solution was to abstain from sex totally as a means of birth control during your fertile time.

I asked my mom, "Did the Rhythm Method work?" She without a beat replied, "No we have 5 kids!" Then my mom burst into her awesome full hearted roaring laughter! I loved my mom's laugh, you would just laugh because she was laughing even if you didn't fully know what she was laughing about. I was discovering a few loopholes to the limited beliefs of our religion with my mom's stories. I began feel ok with the idea of letting go of the rigidness.

When I approached high school something happened to deepen my curiosity that there could be so much more to this mystery of God and the invisible support than the people in my world could ever teach me.

CHAPTER 2

I Just Knew

So fast forward to my beginning a new chapter in my life by leaving Catholic School. I stumbled onto a truth that influenced how I live today. At 13 years old I was about to begin Public High School (hurray!) I was so excited but also very nervous about starting at a much bigger school and being the new girl. So many kids were extremely intimidating to me. However, I was ready for a change. I used to think about how high school would be so much fun and totally different than the seriousness of my experience of Catholic school.

So I ended up in the hospital the day before my first day at Central Columbia High School with very bad pains on my side. The ER Doc told me it was my kidney and I needed to stay home for several days. I told the doctor, "But the next day was my big day!" The Doc said to me, "That is not happening, sorry. Bed rest for you kiddo." I told my mom I HAVE to go to school tomorrow. I was told by my neighborhood friends that the upperclassmen have fun messing with all of the freshmen on the first day sending them in wrong directions when looking for their classrooms. If I go the second day of school rather than the first I will be the only one lost and would definitely stand out as an easy target.

I did not want to stand out! I told my mom I had to feel better the next day. What I experienced that night as I layed in bed was a new kind of experience for me. *I felt it completely and it came from the very core of my body. It came with so much conviction and power.*

I even asked myself in that moment, how do I know this information so clearly and where did this come from? I remember having this little back and forth in my mind as I questioned this "knowing" that I received. The answer to myself in my mind was ... *I JUST KNOW.* I felt as though I was recalling a truth through all of time and space. I knew it was wisdom from a dimension I didn't know yet in this lifetime, and this was a weird thought for me too.

I heard a thought that I could tell wasn't my mine. It was not sassy, not arrogant and not scary. It said, ***"YOUR MIND IS VERY POWERFUL, YOU CAN CREATE ANYTHING YOU WANT WITH YOUR MIND."*** There was a reverence behind this statement that felt like a sacred truth. So I began immediately to repeat, "I am better and feel great, I am going to school tomorrow" I began to picture myself in school the next day through the hallways with all of the students saying hello. I did this off and on all night. No panic. Just practiced what I felt I was to do. I woke up feeling fantastic, pain free, energetic and excited.

Now keep in mind this is 1980. Growing up where I did in Bloomsburg, PA. Only 3 channels on my TV growing up for years. No resources to hear anything but what I was exposed to my little limited world and what I was told. No open-minded books, google or youtube with unlimited information to explore whatever you wanted. This information that came that night was very memorable and impacted the way I live for the rest of my life. I made it to school feeling well on my first day at my new high school and blended in with the rest of the newbies.

That enlightened knowing influenced me in so many ways and I felt in touch with many truths at this age. I began to honor more knowings and inner promptings from this space inside of me. Prior to this experience, I didn't know this deep space within existed. I went from being extremely shy and introverted to being very friendly and outgoing over a very short time. I loved following fashion and took courageous risks for a very small town. I felt completely safe in being authentic and full expression. I liked to crack jokes and have a good laugh with my friends, I really loved people and enjoyed chatting with everyone at this new school.

My parents around this time taught me something that was huge in shaping me into who I am in my views. Again, being shown another perception than my earlier teachings and the idea of there is only one way to God. My parents message struck a chord in me, because this was supremely different from what I was taught in school. Again, hearing more about love and acceptance of everyone regardless of religion. I began to get curious as to what other philosophies exist.

> *EVERYONE IS IMPORTANT IN GOD'S EYES. WE ARE ALL EQUALLY LOVED AND VALUABLE TO HIM. WE ARE ALL GOD'S CHILDREN.*

Beautiful truth

My parents sat me down one day in ninth grade. I was asked to have a seat and it was handled in all seriousness and reverence. I was told;

You are no more important than anyone else. We are all equally valuable to God. Our insides are all the same. It doesn't matter the skin color, religion, culture, or financial status. No one is more important than anyone else.

I have so much gratitude for this foundation I was given. Today I am blessed with friends from all over the world, different beliefs, and different skin colors, different religions. I often think how I could have missed so much in life if my parents had not given me this golden information and if I wasn't given such a love based philosophy.

The Dr. vs. the Hairdresser

I continued to have some more knowings in high school without trying. Didn't give it much thought at the time but I believed and trusted my epiphanies completely. I didn't know why or how they were coming, but somethings I just knew strongly.

I remember telling my then boyfriend who was on course to be a doctor and who was also the valedictorian of his class a year ahead of me one of my philosophies. He enjoyed that he was smarter than most people, including me. He was super competitive in his pre-med rankings when he got to college. I however went a much lesser path in his mind, I had a passion for doing hair and anything glamorous. My parents allowed me go to beauty school during the summers while I was still in high school. I had my cosmetology license by 17 years old. My parents were totally insistent I attend college. So the compromise was to get my cosmetology degree before college during the summers while I was still in high school.

So one day when my boyfriend was teasing me saying he was so much smarter, I debated his statement of superiority by saying something I felt deeply. "I believe we are all equipped with certain skills placed in our hearts by God." "We are predestined to a degree and everyone has gifts, talents and a purpose!" "God didn't send us here with nothing, but we just have to discover our gifts and hone them."

I continued, some people have mechanical minds, some have more scientific, while some people have more creative minds. I believe we can do whatever we desire. God set us up equipped to be successful and our minds are very powerful. I could be a rocket scientist if I wanted to. It may take me longer than you. I am not engineered in my mind that way. I may need extra help and need to study longer hours and work much harder than you. But if it was my passion and believed I could make it happen, I could do it! *It's where we put our focus, our beliefs and the knowledge and success we acquire is wherever we put our attention. We create our results by where we put our focus and can be anything we want,"* said my 16 year old self.

He debated my theory, so I started to quiz him in bacteriology from my beauty school textbook. He was passionate and an accomplished student of the sciences, yet he stumbled, hemmed and hawed. He did not know the answers naturally as he expected simply because in his mind he was smarter. I made my point! He was the top of his class, on track to be a Dr. yet he didn't know what I knew. It was my current focus and area of study. It wasn't HIS focus even though he had so much science knowledge. He just hadn't studied that area of science. I had no interest in being a scientist but I did want to get a 100% on my test.

Now after years of study and life experience, I feel what is in our hearts, our minds is ours to pursue. No limits! What do you desire? What are your strengths and what brings passion? Do you have dreams and goals? What were you told early on? How have things you were told in the past influenced your life and your path up to now?

You can decide *now* regardless of your past, what do you want for your life? Let go of *others* beliefs if they are not your beliefs, or if they limit your ideas of what is possible and who you are. What do you truly want at the core of your essence? That's a Divine spark speaking to you in a language you understand.

God is not loud (lol, sometimes.) It's the small voice that repeats itself. Did you ever think that small voice could be God prompting you? That your desire or a repeated thought you have is for a purpose? It's like God is saying, I equipped you kiddo. Just take that step!! Then the next, then the next.

I was so excited one day when I came across this this quote by Albert Einstein. Totally what I was trying to relay all these years ago in high school to my adorable but smarty pants boyfriend.

> **"Everybody is a Genius. But if you judge a Fish by its ability to climb a tree, it will live its whole life believing it is stupid." ~ Albert Einstein**

We all have our own gifts. Don't try to fit in someone else's box or let someone else define YOU! What is in YOU? You have gifts that no one else can do quite like you do. Be free to discover the beauty of who you authentically are. What do you desire? You matter!

CHAPTER 3

This Ugly Duckling had a Dream, e i e i ooooo!

I accidentally stumbled a few times successfully into the law of attraction without realizing it. I wasn't intentionally trying to do anything with my thoughts but daydream. I understood what I felt about the power of my mind from my experience in going to the ER and making myself well overnight. Against the doctor's prediction that it would take several days maybe a week to be okay. I knew how my beliefs and thoughts had a direct effect on my body and I was well overnight.

I learned from my *knowing* that we can create anything we want with our mind. All throughout high school I felt this. However, I thought it was more going to affect the health in my body, my career, my success and my happiness because of my attitude. I didn't think where I let my mind dwell and if I envisioned something it could influence actual events that seemed out of my control! I discovered how powerful our imaginations are when something I had been visualizing for a couple of years came to fruition. It was simply something I did as a practice to help me to overcome my extreme shyness.

The quiet little girl

Being the youngest of 5 kids who were quite a bit older than me, I spent a lot of time alone while the big kids were off at school. Most of my family time was observing what was happening in my world at home. I tried to chime in on occasion, but my little voice was drowned out amidst the four louder teens and the busyness of my household. My mom had more than she could handle for one person. I don't know how she did it!

My dad traveled often as a National Sales Manager for Singer Sewing Machine when all 5 of us were home. My mom used to say she was the chief cook and bottle washer. My grandmother was overtaken by Parkinson's Disease not capable of caring for herself and was wheelchair bound. Gram was completely dependent on my mom for everything. And then there was of course little me at home who was about nine to fourteen years younger than the rest of my four siblings.

I tended to wait for everyone to make an effort to talk to me. Often no one really heard this tiny little voice and there was always so much going on. In school I was quiet like I was at home. When I got picked on as all kids eventually do, it was hard to do battle. I didn't know how to defend myself because my siblings were so much older, it was like I had three sets of parents. I didn't have the sibling rivalry because of the age difference - and I didn't have any fighting.

Typically you learn your skills in negotiating by interacting or fighting with your siblings for what you want and defending for what is yours. So when kids do what they do and had little digs or shots directed towards me, I felt inadequate in my response.

The opportunity for a fresh start for high school was appealing to me. I really hoped to break out of my little shy girl shell. A fresh start meant maybe I could recreate myself. So I made up my mind, I am going to be cool, popular, have more fun, a new exciting life. I thought of ways to stretch beyond my current comfort level. Another thing I seemed to just know. *Push a little bit each day outside of where I was comfortable and get a little uncomfortable in order to grow.*

I offered those around me mints or gum to kind of break down the walls of unfamiliarity. I would say hello to anyone who I passed. I really had to push myself and round up some courage. I would act how I thought someone who I wanted to become would act. I made an effort each day and talked a little more than I felt like talking. Accepting the fact it's ok to be uncomfortable. And also taking my mom's advice of get involved in as many activities as you can. Next thing I knew, I was actually having fun. Talking to new friends, joining school activities and getting involved to meet new people.

You get the energy of what you give ~

Well I made some awesome friends out of the gate, but had a couple of people who weren't happy I started at my school. I got a steady flow of letters in my locker telling me I was not wanted there and to go back to where I came from. The notes repeatedly said things like no one liked me, and I was fat and ugly. My mind went many places. I was upset and of course I cried. When I figured out who was behind the notes I decided to confront her face to face.

Funny thing happened one day that changed so much for me in my starting to enjoy school more. One of the mean girls was absent for about a week from school. As a result, I was able to talk to more people freely. There was a popular guy who I knew just enough to say hello. I had so much fun chatting that whole week with this popular boy at lunchtime and really connected. He looked me right in the eye the one day and said, "you know you aren't a bitch at all!" I laughed and said, "well thanks?"

I paused a second and thought well that was random. Wondering what prompted that statement I asked, "Why do you say that?" He told me what was being said about me by a girl who knew me from my neighborhood. She told people not to be friends with me, that I was a rich bitch.

The popular boy said he was going to tell everyone I was cool and she was wrong. I found out he also told other kids in the school about how a couple other girls were sending me mean notes to my locker. Interesting thing, how the mean girls didn't want people to be friends with me and did everything they could to hurt me.

The outcome of their efforts to ostracize me and make me small and unlikeable backfired. It unfortunately boomeranged back to them. Because of what they did was people started to shut *them* out. I noticed and the mean girls noticed too.

A lesson for me looking back to this time is....

> *You get what you give, the energy of where you are and what you are putting out to the world. Your experiences are a reflection of the energy you hold.*

From a Spiritual Perspective ~

Situations that challenge us are really an opportunity to bring more LOVE into our lives. It gives us the opportunity to clear and release something within us that is NOT LOVE in our beliefs that we may not even be aware. When the action I chose was to honor myself by addressing the situation head on, I sent out the Universe a message of I deserve respect. I chose to respect myself when I acted in self-care and self-love by addressing the person who wrote the notes.

We are constantly sending out an energetic message. The vibration of what we think, our actions and words we speak is what is returned to us. *There is no judgement of the energy the Universe is receiving, there is no discernement. Only a reflection!*

I was most likely was holding a bit of fear around not being accepted or loved that I attracted the situation in the first place. The universe loves us so much it actually brings things into our experiences an opportunity for us to get us aligned in choosing better for ourselves and to be better.

It's the uncomfortable situations that catch our attention, do you agree? Easy things are just easy things, often we do not evaluate the why when things go right! But what infuriates us, unfair situations, heartbreak, what shakes us up and sends our heads spinning....THAT catches our attention!

Since life is a mirror of the energy and beliefs we hold, in the above example of standing up for myself I had set the tone of self-respect. The Universe said, Ok Donna, got it…... order received of love and respect…....sending back love and respect for Donna.

Daydreams came to life! (unintended law of attraction)

I have always loved to daydream and had a vivid imagination as a kid. While in the 8th grade, I began to pretend in my mind that I was in high school and things were fantastic and was confident! I deeply wanted to move on from being a shy and awkward little girl.

I would lose myself in the same daydream of having fun, letting my mind wander to what it may be like for myself if I were better socially. I would imagine how great it would be laughing, going to basketball games. I even added in there…. Oh, wow you picked me as queen? Thank you! I saw myself getting crowned. I am embarrassed to tell you this story, lol. But I think it will help you understand the power of visualization. Acting as if it's already happening and using your imagination like you did when you were a kid.

I didn't know about the law of attraction. And wasn't trying to create anything but a way to feel better and motivate myself to break out of my shyness and gather courage. Whenever I got insecure, I simply went to my homecoming vision of seeing myself having fun with lots of kids - not really giving it any expectation. Just a way to escape my lack of confidence by replacing my self-doubt with the fun of my imagination. I daydreamed about who I hoped to personify someday. An outgoing confident personality that a homecoming queen would embody. Did I want to be homecoming queen? That would be the icing on the cake for a shy backwards girl who wanted fun loving experiences and to just belong.

My youngest daughter Jadin's favorite story of me is when I was in Catholic School and asked by our priest, "Donna what do you want to be when you grow up?" I said, "pretty." Father burst out in laughter. He meant a job! Jadin lost it hysterically when I told her this and brings it up to me occasionally. I found out Jadin was going to get a T-shirt of me made with my dorky pic from first grade. I felt I went through a very ugly and awkward period. You know there was a time you didn't pick your clothes, or haircut....your mom did. I had 70's fashion, no front teeth and a boys haircut. Ugggg!! So I carried a bit of that ugly duckling in me. So of course the ugly duckling inside of me would enjoy being the homecoming queen.

I had heard in 9th grade there was a certain girl everyone KNEW was going to be our homecoming queen. She truly deserved it. Such a sweet, smart and beautiful girl. Everyone loved her. I was totally buying it, and didn't really think anything more of it than yep …. she is a cinch to get it. So fast forward to my senior year, I truly didn't even have what I was about to experience in my radar. The week of homecoming we had a pep rally in the gym the week before the big game. I was having so much fun dancing with the crowd to the marching band playing. We were cheering enthusiastically for the Blue Jays in anticipation of the big game celebrating our awesome football team!

They began to announce the homecoming court one by one. Shocked in disbelief, my name was announced as a part of about seven girls on the homecoming court. I was really humbled and so very grateful to even be included with these girls. I truly didn't expect to be on the court. I didn't take it very seriously that the queen thing was a possibility at first. I suddenly connected the dots remembering what I would play out in my head occasionally for inspiration to not be so shy.

Part of me began to question a little that this was actually happening. I was like well this is pretty surreal, what is going on here? Is it possible? Also I knew exactly who everyone wanted to be queen and I voted for her too! (please remember I was 17 years old, lol. Hang with me I learned so much from this one experience!)

The night came where the Homecoming Court got to be chauffeured in our own cars with our escort by our sides. We waved to the crowds from the cars decorated with our names scrolled on posters with glitter, crepe paper and tissue flowers. Finally at halftime we were escorted onto the football field. One by one our names were announced at the stadium over the loudspeaker as we made our way to the front of the football field.

There we all stood waiting to hear, there was a pause before the big reveal. I was shocked that suddenly it was my name that was announced as the homecoming queen. That moment in time I was living everything I imagined and pretended it would be when I went to my vision. The magical feeling, the bright stadium lights seemed to have beams through my happy tears, getting crowned, the applause, the hugs and kisses, posing for the newspaper pictures. Part of me was excited and really very honored. Another part of me instantly felt undeserving and badly that my friend didn't get the crown.

This is funny I just had to add, lol. I have a pic of when they announced my name. My look of shock, my jaw dropped and my arms flailed out and punched my escort in the stomach, his reaction to getting banged in the stomach was captured on film. Lol Sorry Roger. I was clearly surprised.

My teenage questioning

My take away from this experience afterwards was, wow! Did I do this? Or did it just happen by coincidence? I spent some time thinking about this the next day. I had the realization of holy crap I am powerful which resonated with me ever since that experience. I really started to ponder, I think our minds may be more powerful beyond what I thought.

I wondered at 17 years old what else don't I know about? So much the people around me didn't know around this topic, was I the only one that knew about this? Who could I talk to about this? I held onto this new lesson and hoped to learn more of the workings that were being revealed in very impactful ways.

What I have learned around Law of Attraction

The law of attraction to me means that the core beliefs you hold, what you focus on, where your mind dwells, your words, thoughts and deeds, visualize regularly in your mind creates the state of the energy and essence of your vibration. Which in turn will create your experiences. Like attracts like with Universal energy. It's really physics and we have the power of co-creating.

"Everything is energy and that's all there is to it. Match the frequency of the reality you want and you cannot help but get that reality."
~Albert Einstein

The idea I would like to talk a bit beyond what you are creating with your words, thoughts and deeds. Our energy also may carry a lifetime of beliefs and experiences. Taking this even deeper is the idea that something someone said or did to us could have impacted us years ago in ways we don't even realize. We hold onto to something energetically that is influencing what we attract to ourselves. And now it becomes a habitual pattern for us.

Deepak Chopra has stated in his book Quantum Healing we have over 65,000 thoughts a day. 95% of those thoughts are repeated every day, like a tape recorder playing the same tape over and over. Do you feel sometimes as if life keeps bringing you more of the same kinds of situations, experiences and you are feeling the same kind of state?

Take a look around you. What are you experiencing? This is a clue as to where your mind dwells in those 65,000 thoughts! The great news is if you don't love it, you have the power to change it and create better for yourself! If you do love things in your life, then by all means keep doing what you are doing!

If we sat with the *why* we feel a certain way around specific topics it could help us to shift into letting go and consciously choosing better and what is true for us.

Asking ourselves with curiosity why do I believe what I believe? Just because we think something does that mean it's true? No, it doesn't. Look at racism. Some people have thoughts such as other races or religions as inferior to them. Is that true? Nope, not at all. We naturally love as children. Just because something is taught to us doesn't always mean it's true, even in schools. I learned this from my Ph.D. holding Education Professor friend Carol that some history that is taught is not accurate.

Let's look at the topic of money. Where did your attitude around money come from? How is your money flow, is it free or lacking? What did you hear growing up? Was it statements such as; I am not made of money, or money doesn't grow on trees. Do you feel tense around the topic of money or maybe you are lucky and feel free? Maybe money excites you and you never worry? Maybe you were raised with an abundant attitude about money. We are all Influenced by our learned experiences.

I spoke with a woman who never worries about money. It always finds her. But love evades her. She feels anxiety around love and not having love. She knows the why. She is of afraid of being hurt again and she knows she holds back when ever new relationships begin. I suggested for her to identify with the freeness she feels with money. If she could tap into that same freedom and trust that love is always in flow to her, she IS love, keeping in mind it's all energy could help her to feel more ease. Choosing to step out of resistance or fear and instead imagine literally jumping fully into that good energy – into the feeling and flow that feels so free. Mimic in her energy how she feels around money. Choosing to trust that love will always find her. And by loving herself fiercely, that love will be reflected back to her.

Just sitting for a bit to understand where we are in our perceptions, in regard to how we feel around certain topics will help us moving forward in making better choices and align with our truth. Letting go of untruths, and letting go of old experiences. Opening to better thoughts, feelings, understanding the why in your belief system and asking yourself.... is it true is very empowering.

Our past doesn't have to be our future experience. We can choose to shift our automatic programming of how we have been navigating life. You can apply this to every topic or belief such as love, happiness, success, and finances.

As Mike Dooley says in his Messages from the Universe, THOUGHTS BECOME THINGS. This is absolutely true! Our thoughts have a direct effect on our feelings. I have learned that the *feelings you have are a clue to the energy you are holding and where your mind has been.* If you don't like a feeling…..ask yourself what have I been thinking? *An undesirable emotion is a call from your heart to listen deeply within.* Look at your circumstances and feeling asking yourself - is this what I want to create? Then ask yourself next….what DO I want to create instead?

You enhance the attraction by being aware of what you are thinking and believing in your everyday life and in your awareness of self. It begins with YOU and being present with in and what is being shown in the world around you.

Be the vibration ~

An example of becoming the vibration of what you want goes many years back for me. There was a time I got into bad habits of being critical of others, complaining, judging, being negative. It's when I was married, my husband and I spent a lot of time early on being negative and complaining. It was our entertainment, I supported his negativity and he supported mine. I remember one day thinking boy everyone is miserable, every store I go to I get a nasty cashier, what's THEIR problem?

When I started reading spiritual books I read about going on a *negativity diet.* Stop complaining, be positive, stop watching negative news, and no gossip. I learned about how to be more responsible and more positive about how we are living, what we are saying, and putting out there affects how we feel. What we are experiencing is a reflection of how we are on our insides. Life is a mirror reflecting back our inner world.

I wanted to try this philosophy and immediately made changes. I told my husband I wanted us to trying being more positive, I explained the ideas around what I read to him. I absolutely started noticing positive changes in my world around me by changing my words to better, a better attitude, I got away from talking negatively about others. I was much more positive!

I suddenly started enjoying the world around me coming across very friendly fun people almost magnetically. Checking out in stores I was greeted with friendly cashiers now, I now seemed to find friendly people who were also positive everywhere I went. I wanted to experience positive people, so I had to be a positive person!

Creative power of the written word and spoken words

So knowing what we now know, you can choose how you want to be in the world. If your words have power….chose great words and declarations. It helps to be prepared when you catch yourself going in a negative direction if you have a tool ready to help you to create better.

Write down some positive empowering statements of what you wish to create in the present tense as if it already exists. Prefacing statements as if you already embody what you desire with words such as "I have", or "I am" when at all possible. The idea is you are speaking about your desires as if they are already here, in the present.

Also beginning affirmations with "I am" is aligning with God. Remember the biblical story of Moses and the burning bush? Where God spoke to Moses explaining when questioning who was speaking. God replied, "I am that I am." "I am," is God. This is one of the most powerful tools of creation. The words you speak following "I am" is creative. Just imagine if you say I am happy, I am blessed, I have the best relationships. I have a waiting list of clients and I am in high demand, business is fantastic!

Try on statements of what how you would love to feel, and see if it makes you feel aligned with what you want, such as:

- I am loving my job, I am appreciated and I am compensated generously for my time.
- I am so grateful and thankful the joy in my world, I love my life.

- Life flows easily for me, I am blessed and I am open to receive all of my good in all ways.
- I am loving my new beach house and the sounds of the ocean fill my soul. (why not, lol.)

Write statements that help you feel good and help you to feel empowered, or your favorite day dream and carry them with you in your pocket or tuck them in your purse or wallet. If your mind goes to worry or not in a good place just stop yourself. And replace those thoughts and instead *read from your list of what you really want your life to be to invite that in! Take a moment to really feel it in your body as well. Begin a new practice of positivity and faith.*

I just happened to be in the basement to grab something and my eye went to a book I read years ago. I felt inspired to turn to a page in the book, The Miracle of Water by Masaru Emoto. The entire book is around the power of your words to bring about change and the affect our lives. Dr. Emoto demonstrates that loving words spoken over water formed beautifully shaped crystals. Conversely when negative words spoken over water the crystallized shapes were not complete or rather quite disturbed in shape.

Dr. Emoto states in the book that the Japanese believe *words have spirit.* What if, right? Think about the creative power behind our words in shaping our own lives if words have spirit.…. really think about this idea… how about the power shaping goodness for *others* with our words.

Omg, look what I did!

Well I came up with a doozie of an example for you about the power of your words a couple of years ago. Big takeaway, it's no joke…. Be careful what you are saying!

I kept saying as I was feeling a bit overworked and exhausted in my career. I was representing a few different manufacturers and traveled a lot. Also on an Artistic Team that designed advanced education curriculum and then I taught that curriculum to other professionals. As well as working in two hair salons in two different states. Oh yes, AND being a single mom caring for my girls and running my home. Even though I completely loved what I did for a living, I asked often when I was feeling run down …. "Universe *please* give me a break, I'd love to have off for a couple of months and just rest."

You know what I attracted within a year after I said that statement out loud over and over and over? A full hysterectomy, I had an abdominal incision to accommodate the removal of a gigantic tumor the size of a 6 month pregnancy, gutted like a fish, staples across my abdomen, no sex and knocked on my butt for 2 months.

I realized I got EXACTLY what I asked for. Ok, lesson learned the hard way - *Be clear and complete in your intention.* I DID get what I asked for and I had 2 months off with my feet up. I said laughing as I was healing and couldn't do anything because I was too weak from blood issues that came from my situation. I realized hey, you know I did ask to be off for a few months to just relax. And I repeated it often. Lesson learned Universe, gotcha! Next time I will make a statement such as can I please have 2 months off, I am adding to my statement …… for fun, feeling awesome, peaceful, with plenty of money, at the beach and drinking margaritas with fantastic people I adore.

The lessons in the spaces ~

I heard Oprah Winfrey say during a show one time that we have 3 defining moments that impact our lives. My high school experience of quickly overcoming sickness with my focused thoughts. And my homecoming moment that I had been visualizing that manifested as a real life experience truly influenced me. Learning about visualization was pretty crazy. All were defining moments discovering how powerful our thoughts and visualizations are in creating our world.

I was so excited to years later when I became aware of entire teachings and books around these truths I just knew at 13 years old. *OUR MINDS ARE VERY POWERFUL!* My innate curiosity seemed to push me on a path become an International Wish and New Heart Movement Teacher,

Energy Empowerment Teacher and Coach, a Reiki Master/Healer and Infinite Possibilities Trainer. I have manifested for years. But I am a forever student and still learning.

Yes, I'm embarrassed of what I was envisioning. The evolved older woman knows how fleeting a title or beauty is and that your inner beauty and being authentic is of greater value toward true beauty. I hope you can see my example of what manifested *visualizing without attachment* with my homecoming story. I didn't need to buy into it lock stock and barrel, I didn't even know that I was creating. I just totally was just having fun and trying to build confidence. They didn't teach THIS at St. Mary's. :)

Chapter 4

It's Not Outside of You

Off to college I went, as I was fulfilling the deal I made with my parents at 14 years old. I decided to pursue a bachelor's degree in Office Administration specializing in Management. I hoped one day to open my own salon and figured I could learn something with a business degree that would support my dream.

Beyond classes with the ultimate goal of graduation, I also found the freedom to be responsible for myself, free of my parents strict rules and supervision. Which meant parties, joining a sorority, becoming a student senator, kickline dance team, and many wonderful friendships. I was loving life and I took a sabbatical from my spiritual side. Life was totally about fun for the next four years. The following stories rekindled my curiosity and got me back on track to discovery. I didn't go searching but I couldn't help but notice some odd happenings. I was receiving communication from Heaven through a feeling, and the coincidence of a significant conversation, and I began hearing and seeing in new ways.

I'm Baackkkkk ~ that voice!

I was very excited about a particular job I saw in the want ads after college. I went to my interview with my soon to be boss. I found her to be a hoot and I was completely entertained with the content of our conversation. During my interview, I observed something happening within my body.

I had a noticeable constricted feeling in my stomach. And I heard that *knowing voice* in my head again. As I listened to this woman comments during my interview, I realized we approach life completely differently. I heard in my mind, *you don't want to work here, you won't be happy.*

I went home laughing at how well the interview went, however I felt clearly this was not a good match. Shortly after my interview I received a phone call from the same woman offering me the job along with a salary about $10,000 higher than the other jobs I was considering. Well the lesson learned here was a pivotal one for me, around going against your gut!

I talked myself into taking the job for the higher salary by saying to myself, "Donna you are such a hard worker, what could possibly go wrong?" I lasted 9 months in that position. The voice was right, I wasn't happy. I knew it immediately within only minutes of listening to the conversation during my interview it was a NO! I heard it in my head and felt my knowing literally *screaming NO* in my body in the first 5 minutes of the interview. I wanted to know more about this undeniable connection that no one talks about. At least no one I knew yet.

I see dead people

During the nine months at this job I had gotten married. One night I woke up around 4 a.m. to run to the bathroom in our new condo. There I was in the bathroom looking out into the living room lit only by the twilight of the moon. I saw the figure of a woman about 3 feet tall, and her image appeared as shadowy and dark. She was wearing a dress and was floating up and down several inches above the floor. She waved hello to me then pointed for me to come the dining room, like she was calling for me to come out to her. I frantically shook my head NO! I rubbed my eyes thinking I am still asleep, surely I must be seeing things!

When she didn't go away, I yelled for my husband. He came rushing in asking, "what's wrong?" I said, "there's a *ghost* behind you look!" He turned on the overhead light looking at me in the bathroom. I could still see her behind him with the lights now turned on. There she was floating and pointing again to the dining room. I could see it wasn't a shadow cast from outside at all, nor my imagination. I pointed out to the living room, "she's still there, LOOK!!" My husband turned around to look and with that she disappeared.

I was so scared and he didn't believe me. I told a few of my college friends who we regularly got together with on weekends about my odd experience, trying to make sense of it. I laughed when my friend Julie told me her dad said, Julie you and your friends have to stop doing drugs. She told her dad, she doesn't do drugs and she was totally sober!

I really wanted answers to whatever the heck this was. I assumed this woman's shadowy figure was evil because the form was dark. I found a medium who was published and well known in Berks County for her contribution to a local Ghost Stories book. She tuned into my situation and told me it was my great grandmother from Ireland on my mom's side. My grandmother wanted me to come sit and talk to her, that's why she was pointing. The medium told me she was there to tell me, "there were greener pastures ahead for me."

Apparently she saw I was not happy with my current job, and wanted to let me know better things were waiting for me. I told this lady that's nice, but can you please tell her that I don't want to see ghosts, I appreciate her reaching out but it scares me.

Now I hear angels!

I was able to leave that job I didn't love and finally got into my passion which was hairdressing. I was fortunate to build a clientele very quickly, and people who I totally enjoyed! One of the things I love about my job is the not only the artistry, but also the connection and abundant relationships we build as hairdressers with our clients. We have clients who bring different gifts to us. Ones who bring such laughter and joy, some bring enlightenment and wisdom, some help us learn to grow our patience and communication skills.

I had one particular client who opened my mind in ways that was totally new information to me. Cindy told me one day that she was descended from a Pow-wow in Berks County. Ok yeah, I didn't know what that was either. It was described to me as a Pennsylvania Dutch medicine woman, a healer. Cindy and I had many a conversations I found interesting.

Cindy excitedly called me at home one night to tell me about a book titled *Angelspeake.* The women authors Trudy Griswold and Barbara Mark were on tv right now, and she strongly urged me to turn on PBS. These two ladies were explaining how we all can learn to hear our angels with ease by doing angel writings.

I was completely glued to my TV and mesmerized. A curiosity rose in me listening to these women. I felt maybe this is safe and I really wanted to try this. There was a method that made a realm of Heaven accessible to everyone? For years I have felt there was more than the black and white version of things from my upbringing. I just didn't know how to go about discovering this. I wanted to feel Heaven and have an intimate relationship, a two way street with God. So I immediately made a donation to PBS and soon received the book.

I ran to my mailbox every day hoping today is the day! Finally my book came and read Angelspeake cover to cover in one day. My first attempt to do what is called an angel writing seemed to produce a writing that seemed a bit generic rather than anything profound. Not personal is what I mean, the message I received could be applied to everyone. I followed the instructions, to pray for protection, write your intention or question, believe and receive. Just allow what pops into your mind without judgement and write what you are hearing.

I did this with dedication for a few weeks to see if anything interesting was going to appear on the page. I always received loving words but I was hoping for a message that I would know I wasn't making it up. Looking back the writings were telling me how much I was loved and came across in old and proper language that didn't sound like how I wrote or spoke at all. The authors wrote that the language could be different than ours and how angels are always positive and loving. I felt it was possible that I was connecting with angels because my self-talk tended to be more critical.

The skeptical side within me questioned, Am I just doing this? Until one day I received a message that said, "Snow will fall Tuesday, blanket the earth." I thought to myself I don't remember reading about any prediction for snow in the forecast this week. I checked the newspaper and confirmed there was no snow expected that week at all.

A few days later I was in the middle of a haircut when I heard client in the next chair say, "oh look at it coming down, it's snowing!" I completely stopped doing my haircut. My eyes were drawn to the huge picture window noticing the gigantic snowflakes whirling with great intensity. The exterior view made us feel as if we were in a snow globe that had just been shaken. My jaw dropped open realizing, holy crap, IT'S TUESDAY!!! I asked the entire salon outloud, were they calling for snow that anyone knows of? Everyone said no, they weren't calling for this.

I realized I was really WAS hearing angels. Not only that, they were right in their prediction! I started to do this several times a week, which helped me hear angels when I *wasn't* writing. This practice helped me develop a stronger and more open connection.

Face to face with an angel

My biological clock was ticking louder and louder. My husband told me he just wasn't ready to have a child yet. We were only about 25-26 years old. Who can blame him, I realize now how young that is and a huge responsibility. I was growing bored of the party scene. What was once a great time had become unfulfilling and was ready for the next phase of my life. I felt a little lost and disappointed, as my husband and I wanted different things in the moment.

I prayed to the angels to help me understand as my tears broke the bubbles in my bath beneath me. I felt I didn't have answers to something that should so simple, *what do I have to do to be happy?* I felt my happiness was on hold but we agreed we would wait until we were both ready. I respected where he was but nonetheless I still felt sad. I finished my bath, dried my tears and I got ready to drive to the mall for a bite to eat. I asked my husband when we were finished lunch if we could stop by the bookstore.

I began to gaze at all the titles looking for a book to catch my attention. Next thing I knew I was approached by an elderly man who greeted me with such vibrancy, he emanated such a beautiful warmth and kindness. I decided to stop looking at the selection of books and take the opportunity to spend some time chatting with this sweet man. He talked with enthusiasm a bit about himself and the job he once had. He next asked what did I do? We continued to talk a little, but it wasn't long until he got to the statement that rang through my entire body.

This man looked me dead in the eye and said, "do you know what it takes to be happy?" I paused understanding this was quite the coincidence, as I just had prayed to the angels with me feeling slightly off track in my happiness just a few hours prior. I thought about his question. I paused and responded honestly, "I really don't know!" I stood noticing his wide smile, his eyes twinkling like he couldn't wait to reveal the answer. I could tell this was a special moment and waited with anticipation as when we are waiting to see the answer to a great cliffhanger in a movie.

He informed me that *happiness comes from within you, not from outside of you! It's not from anyone else or any circumstance. YOU decide to be happy.* His eyes seemed to dance and light up from within as he revealed the answer. We ended our conversation said our goodbyes. I started to browse again, still left with a *well that was crazy* kind of feeling after only a couple of hours before I prayed about that very question.

I turned around to fully thank him and tell him he was an answer to my prayer from only hours ago. It was only a moment since I turned away from his loving gaze.

I have read stories when an angel appears to someone as a human they often seemed to disappear without a trace. And when the person would go to find the person who they had an encounter with to thank them – no one knew who they were talking about. They didn't exist. When I turned around to say something else to the man I spoke with for several minutes, I didn't see him.

I ran to the end of the bookstore and I looked up and down the open hallways. He couldn't have moved that fast. He was elderly and it was only a moment since we spoke. I asked the girl working in the store if she saw where the older man went. The worker said, "what older man?" She never noticed an older man? We were right in front of her for several minutes having my life altering chat while she was behind the register literally only 3 feet from us.

You may be guided to be somewhere or talk to someone. Or someone reaches out to chat with you. Have you ever experienced anything where you thought boy that's a pretty big coincidence! There are no accidents my friends. It's called synchronicity. The timing of this instance was of course within a couple of hours of my pouring my heart out to the angels really caught my attention. And how this special man disappeared into thin air. This was a very impactful moment where I walked away feeling like I was touched by Heaven.

Looking back ~ and Looking within

Things from here really began to unfold in my search for God and my role. My guidance in "knowing" I would not be happy in that job, exercising my free will by taking the job anyway left me with a wisdom I gained that day at 22 years old. When I notice how I feel with in my body or have a thought out of nowhere, I most of the time listen. Little did I know THAT IS HEAVEN, our divine connection!

Our sixth sense comes in thoughts, visions or feelings, and within our body. I was in a habit of looking outside of myself for answers and to think other people knew what was best for me in my 20's. From the logical side of things, the money was the pull for me to take that job. Even though my entire body screamed NO WAY. We often walk through life unawake, not aware and often dismissing what *seems* like self-talk or letting others influence us *against* our inner promptings and higher wisdom.

I did take the job against my inner wisdom. On the bright side, I got the bigger picture and learned something valuable about myself from that experience that impacted me for the rest of my life. It led me in direction of being curious and passionate, to wanting to explore more about how *that knowing* seemed to tell me everything I needed to know in that moment.

My next story I found I could "hear" the invisible realm. Learning how to be still and tune into the higher wisdom speaking. I learned how it's ok to ask questions I would like answered or for guidance. And also, to expect to receive messages from our very own invisible support system. All because my client happened to call me one evening and told me about the Angelspeake book that opened me to possibilities of hearing angels. It is not just for chosen people, we all have the ability to hear it if just we take the time and practice.

The most valuable tools for hearing our Divine guidance exists in our own spirit and body. The difference with recognizing communication from the angels from our own thoughts is the language, the tone, and where we feel it in our minds and body versus our own thoughts. It may seem so simple it's easy to mistake this communication as your own voice. The verbiage from angels is always positive, supportive and loving. Also I find it's very direct and clear. With practice you will see the difference.

The next story taught me *happiness is an inside job*. And also if you ask for help, you will receive help. By identifying my question and pouring my heart out I did get an answer outside of me. But it all began from within. The miracle that day of my angel experience was very special, that man showed me I was heard. Was he an angel or someone who the angels used as an earth angel to deliver a message? The fact he disappeared almost instantly led me to believe he was an angel. Either way is a blessing. Message received!

The wisdom around happiness that was shared in the bookstore that day I have come to learn as a spiritual teacher in years to come. It is absolutely the foundation of life, *it all begins with self.* We decide in every moment how to be and how we choose to look at things. But at 25 years old, that was new information to me and I had allowed life happening outside of me determine my happiness. This certainly was another impactful way to catch my attention. Got it.....***Happiness is an inside job!***

CHAPTER 5

A Real Life Teacher

Very soon after buying my salon and becoming a business owner at 28 years old, I found out I was pregnant with my first child. My daughter Morgan came 9 months after I signed the papers and leapt head first into being an employer. I swear to you, immediately when I looked at the positive pregnancy test results, I said excitedly to myself....it's a girl!

My mom had amazing intuition and 100% trusted her gut feelings in any situation. Yet she stood by her view that psychics were not of God. When I told my mom I think it's a girl, my mother immediately said she felt like it's a girl too. My mom said she was always right with predicting babies. I was curious to know if this intuitive gift ran anywhere within our family history. I had come to understand intuitive gifts seem to be passed down from generation to generation. Kind of like inheriting dimples or freckles. So I asked my mom if this intuitive gift ran in our bloodline somewhere.

My mother excitedly replied, OH YES! And proceeded to tell me about my Irish great grandmother who read tea leaves, not just for family but for people who sought her out. I asked with complete surprisement to this new information, "well was she ever right with what she said in readings?" My mom said, "all the time!"

My mom enthusiastically shared that my Aunt Peg and Uncle Gus had a dream book that had a special drawer where it was kept in the dining room china cabinet. It was brought to the United States from Ireland and had belonged to my great grandmother Sarah Sharky. I was told the family would sit around the dining room table when my mom was little and interpret dreams.

What? A whole world was showing up for me in this moment that I was told was wrong to participate. Learning it was a part of my bloodline and my mother's childhood experience? Excited and confused as to why we never talked about this, now almost in my 30's. I said, "Mom what happened that you think intuition is wrong, or why do you want not want any part of it?" My mom said simply, well the church says it's wrong. I said, "but you experience it!"

I tried to talk more about her contradiction in the way she lived life while having a gift that she pushed away. Church was the ruler of our home and this talk always made my mom uncomfortable, so I let it go. One of the 10 commandments right? Honor your father and your mother. But now I was even *more* curious!

A dance with the devil ~

My special little girl Morgan Sarah arrived July 7 and weighed 7 pounds 7 ounces. I had so many people point out her numbers. 7-7 and 7.7, many were saying you should play the lottery....that's a lot of 7's. One alarming perception that was told to me by a friend who I used to work with, she was from the bible belt in the south. Kathy said, "Donna that child is special, 7 is God's perfect number. She has a special purpose for God, so you better be careful the devil will try to get her."

Well THAT is a horrifying notion for a newly overprotective mom! I didn't believe my friend initially, and I laughed it off. I liked the thought that my daughter was special and had purpose for God, but not that we were going to have to outrun the devil. It didn't help my paranoia that my daughter did some serious projectile vomiting like the exorcist as a newborn.

My friend Kathy had worked with me a couple of years at the salon after I was first married before I purchased the business. I credit Kathy with a life changing moment for me that opened my eyes to a new truth. That

I am loved and important to God. At the time I was still feeling some unworthiness from my early teachings but was proven wrong in one just one moment. All because my friend took a minute to help me in a different way than I have been exposed to in all of my 25 years.

My husband had decided to try Insurance Sales as a career. He was having challenges in getting a sale. I was telling my friend so much was riding on his getting a sale and he needed to prove himself. There was a possibility that he could be let go from his position.

Kathy was a gorgeous tall thin 20 something, always beautifully and perfectly dressed, decorated with pearls and her adorable southern drawl. She said, "Donna let's get down on our knees and pray to Jesus." I laughed and said, "Kathy Jesus doesn't hear my prayers. I've tried." She heard me out, and said Donna Jesus is your friend, He loves you!

Well I was certain I would be struck down with lightening right there in the salon if I thought Jesus was my friend. I felt God was far so away and the likelihood of having my prayer picked was like one of those duck pond games you see at carnivals where all the ducks are floating around a circle of water. God would reach in and pick a prayer amongst all of the praying people. Ok, this one will be answered today!

Kathy insisted we kneel right there behind the salon reception desk waiting for our next client. She took my hands in hers and she spoke out loud for Jesus to come to my husband and me, to help him with a sale and could God please let me know soon that he is helping us. We literally spoke together "Amen" and the salon phone rang loudly bursting through the silence. We were still hand in hand and knees to the floor. She let go of my hands, me still on my knees....Kathy answered the phone. Kathy looked at me and said Donna, it's your husband. I thought she was totally joking.

I answered the phone, low and behold it WAS him. It was not only him, he had news......*he got a sale!* I of course was stopped dead in my tracks at the timing of this call. *Wow, I was heard and shown I am loved and important.* So when my friend Kathy mentioned the thought regarding 7's and Morgan I laughed. But deep down there was a tiny bit of - what if she's right? I learned next how I gave her statement more weight than I realized. (*The energy we hold creates our experiences.*)

My daughter of course was 100% my focus and the best thing that had ever happened to me. I had never in my life experienced a love this pure, Morgan filled my soul completely. However, it wasn't all rosy. My daughter had severe esophageal reflux, taking her to Hershey Medical Center to see a Pediatric Gastroenterologist. She cried about 8 hours a day, projectile vomiting constantly, and rarely slept for a newborn baby. When we sat her up in our arms she felt relief. Eventually we discovered what we called a "buzz seat" that my daughter seemed to enjoy. Morgan had a seat that vibrated in a way that soothed her instantly.

I put Morgan in her special chair one morning and we did our usual playtime. We were surrounded by her toys, her books and also a pair my slippers I had taken off. I watched in disbelief as I witnessed my one of slippers rolling over BY ITSELF about 12 inches from me! A complete turn, flipped two times right in front of my eyes! During the last few days we also experienced boxes of cereal that seemed to be just whirled of the top of the refrigerator where we stored them. Not just once but several times. One minute on top of the fridge, the next thing we would hear a little thud only to find a box on the floor almost in the next room.

Kathy's story about the devil and my daughter started to creep into my mind. Later that night I had a dream that Morgan was being levitated about 3 feet out of her crib by an invisible demon out to get her. In my dream the clock radio in her room turned on all by itself playing music while she was being levitated. The absolute panic I felt in this dream seemed so real, I remember praying in my dream how do I protect my girl? All of a sudden Morgan began to cry for real! I was never so happy to be woken.

Oh THANK GOD it was only a dream! Phew! Relieved to pick up my sweet little baby, I held her close to my chest trying to calm myself down. The sweet sounds of her cooing as she took her bottle got me out of my crazy feeling. As I began to burp Morgan, what happened next seemed like my nightmare was coming to life.

Morgan's clock radio turned on all by itself. Scared out of my wits, I thought this shit is getting real! I turned on the light in the nursery to check it out, surely I must have accidentally turned the alarm on. Nope... the alarm was off...the radio was off...yet the radio was still playing. I unplugged that clock and brought my daughter into our bedroom. No way was my girl spending the night in THAT room without my protection!

What was I going to do about this? Call a priest? I didn't feel the priest at our church would have the answers I needed. My client who told me about angelspeake also had been telling me to call this woman she thought I would enjoy who was a spiritual teacher and facilitator.

The next morning after the clock radio incident with no idea where to turn, I decided to give this woman Cindy had told me about a call. I made an appointment and was hopeful to find some answers around the strange happenings in my home.

It's just the energy of your focus ~ you are attracting what you fear

I drove up to Nancy's long driveway out in the beautiful mountains in Antietam PA, only about 20 minutes from my home. I saw before me a very old stone farm home, it wasn't scary at all. To the contrary it was so inviting. The sounds of the leaves rustling in the tall majestic trees, the daisies seemingly dancing back and forth around her historic stone home created a welcoming and peaceful greeting for this nervous girl.

Nancy was a beautiful woman maybe about 20 years older than me. The warmth of her smile, her long dark hair and dress reminded me of a Native American woman. She opened her arms and immediately greeted me with a hug. Nancy was very well spoken, intelligent and a deeply wise vibe.

I don't remember exactly where I began with her, but through Nancy's questions about why I was there, I was quickly informed how I was creating my experience.

> *I was attracting what I was fearing. I attracted my experience because it was just where I was putting my focus. If I stopped making fear my focus, it would stop.*

Nancy told me to focus on God and connecting to the light. This was all so new, but it made so much sense. So the devil wasn't after my daughter? She laughed and told me no, it's just the energy of what I was focusing on. I needed to focus on the Light. She told me as I keep focusing on the Light and Love of God, making God first and praying, meditating and focus then that's what I would attract.

Nancy told me out of the gate, what she was about to tell me was HER truth. If whatever she was telling me didn't resonate with me then that's simply not MY truth. I felt so completely understood for the first time ever, I also believed it was ok to have different beliefs. She answered so many of my questions that no one seemed to be able to my entire life. I was looking for ways to be closer to God what seems like forever that had gone unfulfilled. I never had met anyone who was just open, loving, wise and accepting without judgement. Love emanated from this woman palpably.

Her teachings of love, acceptance, and peace seemed far from bad teachings to me. I left my appointment with an exhilaration, peaceful and felt loved by God, deserving and equipped with new ideas that were so beautiful and resonated with me to my core.

Over many sessions I was taught how to meditate and be open to hearing God. I began to feel God's presence by being still and watching the world around me to receive Divine messages. God is always with us and we are not separate was a new concept for me to grasp. Everyday I saw little miracles unfold. Things became fun, and I would just be wowed by understanding the Universe was speaking to me. The Universe speaks to us all, we just have to be present and know how to understand the messages and language.

Nancy was my very first spiritual teacher, she taught me so much so quickly. She walked the walk 100%, 24/7. What an example of unwavering faith and her beautiful Divine connection. Her amazing manifesting stories where she created what she needed so very easily by just asking Spirit, listening within, trusting and allowing. So simple what I learned, really I could have stopped there. We really tend to make this process much harder than it has to be.

Nancy told me at a session one time that I would be a spiritual teacher someday. I had definitely wanted to know more and keep growing, but how could I be a teacher? I know nothing I told her. She said you will.

CHAPTER 6

Your Body Has Messages

This one thought, the body has messages for you seemed a little farfetched to me at first. This one piece of information can really be enlightening in regards to your health if you are open to the idea. Simple everyday illnesses such as a sore throat or an upset stomach can be a message for you about things you need to look at happening in your life.

I experienced a lot of sore throats as a young child. Nancy told me that means be not speaking your truth. Or in some cases it can be finally for letting your voice be heard in big way like a huge outburst during an argument when all of the repressed energy of what you have not been saying finally comes up to be released. Just thinking about the idea of losing your voice is not a hard one to figure out. Ask yourself where you are losing your voice? Where do you feel you can't say what you need to say? What have you not been saying for fearing the results if you expressed your feelings?

Another common one I observed with my children is if they were not looking forward to something at school they would get a stomach ache. The stomach area is your *power center* or also referred to as your solar plexus chakra. Usually there was something where my girls felt out of their power or fearful around. Such as a test they weren't prepared for, or maybe a conflict with another kid at school. It must have been funny being my kid, mommy I have a stomach ache. Ok, I'm sorry doll. So tell me what's going on at today at school? How are things going with the kids at school? Trying to get to the root of where they were feeling out of their power.

The word "disease" can be broken down into dis- ease. Not being at ease. If you haven't heard of Louise Hay, I highly suggest any of Louise's books to help heal any area of your life to create better for yourself in countless ways. Her books really break down to self-love and care. The power of letting go and healing situations from your past that you may have been holding in your physical body and/or energy body. This repressed energy can be seen in your in your life experiences or in health issues. You draw situations into your experience for you to become aware of the energy you are holding and to make changes in your perspective to heal the energy that needs to be let go. Taking the opportunity to release energy what is not love energy or of God.

We all have unconscious thoughts or beliefs (meaning we may not even be aware of them) that influence us in our daily lives. Louise Hay's books show us how to look at our life experiences that have influenced us and how to heal or let go of a hurt or wound with love and a different outlook by focusing on new thoughts and perceptions using positive affirmations.

I bought two Louise Hay books out of the gate when Nancy introduced me to this idea of the mind, body, and spirit connection. Healing your Body A-Z is a quick reference book where you can look up ailments showing up in your body. Heal Your Life contains very easy to understand concepts about how underlying beliefs and what we are holding within us is manifesting in our lives. It can manifest in our relationships, money, health, wellbeing or affect our self-esteem.

I read with curious interest about how we can empower ourselves to change and heal different areas of our lives by understanding what is happening in our present world. Our experiences are attracted by the core of our thinking and beliefs. We can empower ourselves to change what we are experiencing into more of what we desire by using positive affirmations to help shape our thoughts and language which produce better feelings. Which has an effect on our energy therefore changing our experiences. Funny how when I read new information at the time delving into this new in concept, could it be?

Years later I now help people everyday to understand what is at the core of their thinking by listening carefully to their words and feeling into their stories. We can change to a new story and create miracles when we align with understanding our past, have the willingness to change, and taking loving care of ourselves. Which sometimes self-care means standing up for yourself or forgiving an act of a person who hurt you. Not just all gushy this spiritual stuff. But believe me you win by digging deep and doing the work. It's the most loving act you can do for yourself is to reclaim your power and tap fully into the power and love of God/Jesus/Source/the Universe above all else.

Healing core beliefs will have moments where it means dealing with the things that don't feel great about the past, sitting with the uncomfortableness and unpacking it for clarity and truth around it. To take the time to do this is empowering yourself to shift. There are times making loving and aligned choices for yourself may not please others. Which takes some courageousness on your part. But in time you will see the benefit of choosing YOU by the positive things that come from releasing ways of being or thinking that no longer serve you.

Louise Hay has not only been an inspiration to millions worldwide, but she owned one of my favorite publishing companies and the house of the authors who inspire me, Hay House Publishing. Interesting as I was writing this chapter I had been reconnecting with Louise Hay and her teachings that were a foundation of my studies years ago. As I wrote this chapter connecting with all the beauty Louise Hay taught, she gently passed the same week. I want to thank Louise Hay for her loving grace to this planet and the millions she has helped.

Nancy had told me Louise was diagnosed with advanced stages of cancer years ago and was able to heal herself through positive affirmations, nutritional cleansing, and therapy. This was the first I ever had heard of such a thing and felt her story was inspiring, but didn't embrace the idea around this fully just yet. I bought the book to explore this concept, opened my mind to the possibility and thought well let's see. It seemed far fetched and out there, but who am I to judge? I have learned so much already by opening my mind but a part of me was afraid to let go of "normal" thinking.

Fast forward 20 plus years, this has totally grown into my normal every day practice. Looking at the messages behind what is showing up for not only myself but my family and friends. I soon began to understand that the images, words or feelings I was being shown and the chakra I was working on at the time had relevance. A whole new level of awakening began. Your bodies do indeed have messages.

Mommy I don't feel so good

Have you ever noticed if your child is to get sick it somehow strikes right as you are totally exhausted and can't wait to lay your head down on the pillow. At least this is what was true for me when my kids were young. My little cutie came in right after I had just laid down after a super busy day and couldn't wait to feel the coolness of the sheets, my soft pillow and the stillness of the night. My body just began to transition to relaxation when I heard Morgan next to me in very sad and scared voice, "Mommy, I don't feel so good."

The glow of the TV shed enough light in the room to see the tiny shape of her small frame, Morgan looked very concerned. She vomited right there on my light tan carpet what looked like blood, only having the backlight of the TV still on for me to see. I totally panicked for a second, OH MY GOD my child is vomiting blood!

I got my head together and thought wait a minute, we had been out to dinner that night and Morgan ordered spaghetti with meat sauce. I ran over to turn on the light after she stopped. Yep, it was the pasta. It must have not digested well but I was relieved it was nothing like the worst scenario in my mind. The vomiting continued very violently about 3 more times, it seemed she may have gotten food poisoning. Uggg, my poor little girl. Morgan was scared and begging me to stop this for her. Like I could do that, if I could I would! I remembered....wait... maybe there IS something I could do. It's worth a shot, what do we have to lose?

I remembered this new concept that there is an emotional underlying component to an illness. So without hesitation I ran to my bookcase and grabbed my Louise Hay's book Heal Your Body A-Z. I remember hearing Nancy say that when you have a small child you can be a proxy for them. Meaning you can speak on their behalf, do the action *for* them by setting your intention and asking Spirit for permission and their highest good.

I looked up *"vomiting"* and it said that the probable cause in thoughts was the **violent rejection of ideas, fear of the new.** Suddenly my mind went to events that transpired earlier in the evening. Right before bed my husband told Morgan she was no longer allowed in our bed and she was only allowed in her bed. She was a big girl at over 3 years old and her coming over to our bed had to stop. I didn't agree with him but he was my husband. You know how you are supposed to be a united front in front of the kids.

I actually enjoyed when Morgan came into our bed. I slept better knowing she was safe with me. She didn't have the knowledge or maturity to communicate how the news of staying in her bed made her feel. After all she was a child and her parent was giving her an order, what choice did she have? We as children often don't feel we have choices or control of a situation, or we may get in trouble.

I discovered in the book Healing A-Z the thought creating the vomiting for Morgan could be – "a new idea may not be digesting well." This completely resonated with me with the events that happened earlier. I informed Morgan I was going to try something to help her to feel better.

I asked God and the healing angels to please come help my daughter, and I asked Morgan's Higher Self's (that part of her which is Divinely connected to truth, to God) permission to let me act on her behalf and prayed to God to let me be her proxy.

I began repeating out loud the new thought pattern affirmation that went along with nausea and vomiting. "I digest life safely and joyously, only good comes to me and through me." I repeated this quietly in her little ear a few times, repeating it over her, my hand resting on her to comfort her. It worked almost immediately. Morgan had vomited for the last time and I witnessed her transition to a calmness and relaxation in her body as I spoke the words. She was so tired and quickly drifted off to sleep. I was totally relieved and also wowed by this experience.

The funny outcome of all of this whole ordeal, Morgan got to sleep with me. That little genius! She got her way. A tiny powerhouse creating what she wanted and her body was communicating really with me being awake to the message, as she was too young to look at the deeper meaning. Another note is little kids are very open to ideas like this, as they don't have all the doubts and reservations we do as grownups.

The next day I was in complete amazement of what I experienced learning about the power affirmations and my girl was totally fine. How awesome to have another tool and understanding of how the universe works with us and through us. And how our body can communicate where there are deeper emotional things for us to look at to heal and what's is troubling us.

My quest that I had as a young child in wondering if there was more than what I was taught in my early years was unfolding before my very eyes with more and more experiences.

You matter! Don't forget YOU!

I was in my 30's when I found a lump on my breast. I was proactive and called my gynecologist immediately. He saw me pretty quickly in his office that week. My gynecologist treated this with urgency and ordered a mammogram to be done with in just a few days.

I met the most adorable woman who happened to be my technician for my mammogram. I was very nervous, I never had experienced anything like this before. This lady was a strong but yet a sweet and funny lady from the south. I feel like someone from the south could swear at me up and down and it would still sound charming to me. She treated me with such grace and compassion, she was very tapped into the thoughts that were swimming in my mind and distracted me with her humor.

After she performed the mammogram she locked eyes with me when she popped back into the room. Her previously light hearted and jovial demeanor quickly changed to a very serious tone and expression. Honey, I do this for a living and just want to tell you don't let this go. If they say there is nothing wrong and they are telling you that you are ok, don't listen! Insist on an ultrasound or further testing. It wasn't clean edges it was branching out some, saying it without saying it to me. She looked me dead in the eye with great intensity and said for me to keep on my doctor...that this was very important and she repeated to me again, *Don't let this go!*

So knowing there was a message behind the this, I called Nancy my spiritual teacher when I got home and asked her the spiritual meaning of breast cancer. She said it means you are nourishing everyone but yourself. Because breasts are for nourishing babies and life giving. Well I knew there was truth behind that statement, I never put myself in any equation. She told me I needed to really love myself more and make myself a priority. Take time and be present with myself. Do kind and thoughtful things for myself like I do for everyone in my life.

Nancy also gave me ideas to do as visualizations, and I looked up Louise Hay's affirmations towards a better thought regarding healing breast cancer and I had found a few good affirmations online as well. Nancy informed me this was the Universe giving me a chance to change things. It was my wake up call to dedicate time and energy to myself as a priority, don't forget me!

So daily I took a moment to really fully enjoy my morning coffee and "me" time. Appreciating gazing at the beauty of the sun which I remember loving even as a child. Always loving that peace of tapping into the sun's warmth seemed to have a calming effect to me for as far back as I can remember.

I took more bubble baths, added candles and put on music that made me happy. I would meditate to connect to God and the angels. Many times a day I visualized Divine white light around me and within me. I would envision that Light shrinking the lump to nothingness daily every chance I got. I would picture an unhealthy cell in my mind and watch it get smaller and smaller and smaller until poof, it was gone in my vision. Kind of like aiming a laser in a video game pulverizing and shrinking the lump into nothingness.

I carried around an index card all the time in my back pocket that I had written and filled with affirmations that resonated with my being healthy and well. Whenever I got scared I pulled that card out of my back pocket. In between clients I would read those statements and repeat them over and over in my mind and filled myself with God's healing light. Instead of feeding my fear, I invited in God and stood in His power which is THE power.

I could never seem to remember all of the affirmations. I would go into a panic and my mind went totally blank not being able to recall them, so that's why I carried them with me. And I believe pen to paper creates an energy and vibration that resonates what is written, another benefit of why I carried that wellness vibration with me. This was too important to half ass it or not to commit and focus on myself.

My doctor did tell me in the results of my testing there was a questionable abnormality and I was to get a mammogram every 3 months for the next year to keep an eye on any changes in the lump. So the next mammogram I had the same lovely woman as my tech. She remembered me. She came out from behind her barrier that keeps her safe from the exposure of the mammogram and entered back into my room. The look on her face and her stammering in her loss for words for a minute as she walked towards me got me really nervous.

She said to me, "WHAT DID YOU DO?" I was unclear what she was asking me, I replied, "what do you mean?" She said *it's gone (then a silent pause and just staring at me perplexed)... it's gone honey,* it SHRUNK! I have NEVER seen that in all of my years she told me. What I saw last time in your mammogram has almost completely disappeared to nothingness, it's the size of the point of a pin. Donna that never happens. WHAT DID YOU DO? You had to do SOMETHING! I told this woman what I had dedicated myself to doing spiritually, and how I shifted to include myself in the people I nurture!

Painful to See

This journey is always "eye opening," lol. My next story involves not being able to open my eyes to daylight one morning. It was my day off, so I got out of bed early on a Wednesday to get ready for the gym. I did the first thing I normally do which is to let in the gorgeous sunshine. I opened my blinds to the most clear day not a cloud in the sky. I felt a searing pain when I opened the blinds and my eyes couldn't handle the bright sunlight. I pulled down my room darkening shades to block the sun and yelled for my husband.

I could not open my eyes for even a split second as it would result of horrid pain. I tried warm compresses, then cold compresses. Even prying my eyes open a slit to put in eye drops thinking maybe that would soothe my eyes. Nothing was helping and the pain was off the charts. We called my doctor who referred us to a specialist who saw me the same morning. I joked this must be what a vampire feels like, because in old movies they act like daylight is painful.

I was told by the Doctor that I had a cold in my eyes. I did not know that was even possible, and was relieved it was nothing major but very odd. The doctor prescribed to me antibiotic eye drops. I sat in darkness not allowing any light in for about a day. I did manage to get a call into Nancy as to the deeper meaning behind this so I could heal it quicker. I knew by this point this was no joke your body talking to you after all of my experiences.

Nancy asked me, *"what's painful for you to see?"* Because that's where my problems were in this moment, it was painful for me to open my eyes to "see". Yes it can really be that easy. It makes sense doesn't it? She asked what do I have a problem with when I look at it, what is causing me pain to look at in my life? I said it two things come to mind immediately, I can't discern just one over the other. I am not happy in my marriage, and I am no longer happy owning my salon. I feel stuck in both.

This was "eye opening" once I sat with the truth of this, I also followed Nancy's advice in *talking to my eyes*. I know this sounds crazy, right? Dialoguing with your eyes? This was new to me talking to the ailing body part. I thought, well she hasn't led me wrong so far.

I felt clear in what we spoke about as to the issues, so I took the time to say, "Thank you eyes for bringing me my message, I got it!" "I will look deeper into this message, since I have grasped the message I am asking for the pain to leave now." "Please eyes release the pain." Immediately the intensity started to diminish, later that day I could relax a lot more. The next day was like it never happened. All was well. And of course I eventually in time moved on from both my marriage and being a salon owner. It was a process, but I stopped being in denial and opened to the truth of what my body was bringing to my attention.

CHAPTER 7

Universal Energy 101

I remember when I first heard about Reiki was at my grandmother Criqui's funeral. I was 21 years old and had just graduated from college. My brother Mike and I drove to Philadelphia from Bloomsburg, Pennsylvania. On the way I was thinking about the all of the family who would be at Gram's funeral. My Uncle Jack was so much fun, he had an incredibly dry sense of humor. He always had a smirk on his face looking at life through the lens of great humor and sarcasm, always ready to crack his next joke. I saw a side of my parents I enjoyed to watch, really letting go of their cares having fun with my Aunt Jeanie and Uncle Jack. I would enjoy listening to their jokes and laughter having cocktails in the living room.

Aunt Jeanie and Uncle Jack's daughter Jeanie was a beautiful blonde and a genuinely kind and fun natured. I looked up to Jeanie as a little girl and a few times slept over at her place when we visited my Gram in Philadelphia. I thought it was so awesome to have a younger grown up who always talked to me on my level.

After the funeral we were gathered around the lunch table chatting. The conversation turned to talking about my Uncle Jack getting debilitating migraines and someone asked how he was feeling? He said Jeanie had been giving him reiki and it he wasn't having problems with the migraines anymore.

He explained how these migraines would knock him down and he would lose time at work. That is until Jeanie would come over and do reiki on him regularly. No one at the table had heard of reiki so Jeanie began to explain what it was. I don't remember a lot about her description except is was a form of hands on healing. I do remember questioning her, and she most likely decided the best way to answer to our questions is for us to experience reiki for ourselves. So she walked over to us very calmly without a word placed one hand on my shoulder and her other hand on my brother Mike's shoulder who was sitting to the right of me.

Jeanie just smiled, continued to talk have a lively conversations with everyone at our table all while her hands were rested our shoulders. I noticed where her hand was got very hot. Much more heat than a typical body temperature of someone touching you. We stayed until the lunch was over, then my brother and I left Philadelphia to head back to Bloomsburg which was about a three hour ride.

We hit about half way home, I realized something odd. It had been about 3-4 hours since Jeanie had placed her hands on us, I looked at my brother Mike and said to him, "it feels like Jeanie's hand is still on my shoulder." Mike looked at me and said, "yeah me too." I had thought I was imagining things but the fact that my brother was feeling the same thing? This experience stuck with me for years.

Many years later a friend of mine told me she was taking a reiki class. I asked Becky if the class was open to more people. I had been feeling a strong interest to take learn reiki. The following story happened maybe about 6 months before the reiki class came to my attention, but now I know this experience was meant to catch my attention to explore an energetic healing. Little did I know this door would be my biggest gift into experiencing God's energy and hearing communication with our invisible support system because I ventured down this road to energy healing.

Gram's message

One night after putting Morgan into her crib I laid in bed to read. I had just gotten comfortable and lost deeply into a book when I felt like someone sat on my shins on top of the comforter. I kicked the blankets a little to loosen them. I said to myself, Donna you must be really tired because you are losing it thinking someone is sitting on your legs. Only to feel it again a few minutes later. I kicked the blankets again with deliberate annoyed force this time. It happened to me three times. I started to get nervous and would pray for all of our protection because I still went "old school" and went to my fears assuming this experience was bad.

This was still new to me, I had only been seeing my spiritual teacher for a fews months. I would handle things totally different now. And in our house present day my girls and I have weird things happen in front of our eyes, we look at each other and laugh. Even their friends will mention things as they happen, and they just know that's how it is in our house. It doesn't scare me now and the girls are used to odd happenings. I was still at this stage assuming the invisible was evil, not that it could be just someone reaching out who just wants to say hey!

I made it through the night, it stopped after I prayed for the leg thing to stop. I thought Donna I'm sure you imagined it, you were really tired I told myself. It came time for bed following the same routine the next evening. I got cozy and it happened again. I very strongly kicked the comforter saying, NO, stop!

Third night I went to bed and this time this person was like ok girl, YOU WILL PAY ATTENTION TO ME! I felt a BOOM on my legs. Like an invisible person took a running leap and sat with all of their might on my legs and THIS TIME it made a BIG DENT in my covers. I could see a butt print form in front of my eyes on my legs on my thick fluffy comforter.

Thud, thud, thud, thud, thud was the sound as I frantically ran downstairs saying there is a ghost upstairs, there's a ghost upstairs! My husband's reply was….see this is what happens when you open yourself up to this stuff. You need to stop meditating. I was wondering if his comment was right, I need to talk to Nancy but it was 11 p.m. I would call her first thing in the morning.

At 9 a.m. the next day I called Nancy and was so relieved she answered. She sounded so calm to my amazement as I explained what happened. She replied as if it's not a big deal at all saying, "oh someone is just trying to talk to you." (Ohhhh, is that all it is?) Nancy advised me to just meditate and ask who it is and what they want. I said, "ummm.... No way!" She really wanted me to put myself in a vulnerable position and ask the ghost who it is? This was like putting myself in the middle a horror movie in my eyes. Nancy finally said, "ok how about I am with you when you meditate, come see me and I'll guide you through." That was a much better plan.

I arrived to Nancy's first thing the following day. We chatted for a bit sitting in her very serene healing room surrounded by those majestic trees. I was calmed by the sweet melody of the birds and watching them scurry past the window. Once I seemed comforted in her space, Nancy asked are you ready to get started? I said ok, but can I please use your bathroom first? She said sure.

When I got into the bathroom I silently poured my heart out to God. I had a big conversation with God, Jesus and the angels right there in Nancy's bathroom asking to please protect me. Then I asked God is there anyway Nancy can do this for me? I really don't want to do this! Trying to round up a little courage I took a deep breath then exited the bathroom into the healing room. Nancy said to me without a beat, "God told me you were nervous and I should do it for you." She was amazing.

Nancy sat in her chair, got comfortable closed her eyes and took some deep centering breaths. I sat directly across from her with anticipation awaiting to see who this was. The look on Nancy's face and the smile I could actually feel as she tapped into something very beautiful.

She said she saw woman who just emanates love, she is an older rotund woman with a beautiful, beautiful heart. I already started to know who she meant, but I let Nancy continue without interruption. She proceeded to say she says she is your mom's mom. Yep that's who I was thinking. My gram Parpart. Gram's message for me was that she was here to help me with my gift. Nancy next asked me if I wanted to talk to Gram. Well, of course I wanted to!

I asked what is my gift? I had no clue what she could even mean. My gram said this is for me to find out, allow it to unfold but she will be here with me as it does. Gram also told Nancy about how I saw her after she passed away while I was riding on my school bus. And how she waved to me and no one believed me. This was ABSOLUTE confirmation. How would Nancy know this from 23 years earlier?

She also informed Nancy how I had a near death experience in our pool. I said no I didn't. I was fighting Nancy, lol. But she continued with more detail that was dead on. She said when I was little I was stuck under the water and couldn't find my way to the top of the water. My mom didn't notice me struggling and I saw the white light. I said, "Oh my God that was THE white light?" I did see a white light while I was under the water.

I remember turning in the water and not knowing which way was up. I was learning to hold my breath and did a turn in the water. I lost my bearing and was panicking because I was running out of air - I was waiting for my mom to notice. Nancy said my guardian angel thrust me to the top of the water. I did remember I wasn't sure how I was suddenly on top of the water but finally was getting air.

I felt so blessed for this new information and now I told Gram outloud I welcome her visitations. I also connected the dots a bit after the session that day, I happened to be reading a book on Healing with Colors. I was curious about healing because of my experience with my cousin Jeanie.

As I read the healing with colors book one day during Morgan's nap, I could feel a warm pulsing energy in and around my hand. It traveled like an energetic wave flowing up my arm and into my shoulder. I held out my arm for a bit to connect with my gram and allowed the experience. I could feel an immense love that moved beyond my hand – expanding throughout my arm and moving into my heart. Realizing the timing of making herself known during me reading this book, she giving me a clue healing could possibly be my gift.

First day of REIKI level 1

I think back to how I really jumped in with both feet into reiki with the only understanding was it was the ability to heal. And how my cousin laid her hands on me and I could feel her hand hours later in same spot - even though we were a in separate cities hours later. I felt such excitement moving forward with my training but I was afraid at the same time. I battled fears questioning would the church and my mom approve of reiki? I told myself if anything seems scary I'm outta here!

I was relieved when my teacher Carol opened the door to greet us. She was a very soft spoken woman with beautiful auburn bouncy ringlets around her lovely warm face. Once I deemed Carol safe, I began to take in the room where we would spend the next two days with peaceful spa like music playing in the background. We all introduced ourselves to break the ice until precisely 9 a.m.

The day would begin with the history of reiki, and how important it is to embrace the honor the energy and the intention to be of service. We were to always approach this practice with the highest reverence. We learned the word reiki means universal life force energy.

Very simply some history, I was taught Dr. Usui was a Tibetan Monk. A student one day asked him what healing method did Jesus use? Not knowing an answer, after much investigating and travel Dr. Usui was still searching for answers. He had a miraculous experience during a 21 day fast and discovered the healing modality of reiki, 3 more miracles followed coming down from the mountain where he fasted.

After the history lesson and other important info, the next segment of our agenda would be receiving what's called an *attunement*. This clears us of our blocks to the Universal energy, helping us to be more of a clear channel for healing and being of service. And we were told after each attunement we would be practicing hands on with actual volunteers throughout the two day class.

I felt a little bit nervous for the attunement, why I wondered? It was only my fears mind you, all the thoughts came rushing to my mind of "this could be wrong." I didn't know what was happening with my eyes closed, all I could hear was very purposeful breathing like releasing in yoga.

Getting out of my head and into the moment I began to relax. It seemed like a beautiful light show while my eyes were closed. I saw some purples and greens swirling in my mind's eye during the process. Like a flow of morphing colors continuously changing patterns kind of like a lava lamp. A very trippy.... yet a very holy experience. I knew from meditation and Nancy educating me as to the colors, purple was intuition your third eye opening, and green was healing.

The important facts for us to keep in mind as we conduct a reiki session was that WE are not doing the healing, we were to keep our egos out of the session. We were to remember we are a simply a conduit for the energy to flow. It's universal life force, chi or what the universe is composed of. Basically God's energy. In class we were told it's Divine energy going to exactly where it is needed. And the Divine Intelligence knows exactly what a person needs and where to go, really we just need to show up and be willing to be of service.

In our daily lives we can often create and hold energy blockages in our body. The blockage can result in pain, weakness or illness, also lingering emotions that trouble us. As I said in the last chapter of this book about your body has messages to communicate with us as a tool. Reiki provides a non-invasive way to move and release any blockages or pain to be in full flow and support of the Universe.

Say for instance someone said or did something that hurt you emotionally in some way, you may store this energy in your back area. Back is your support system. Lower back generally is worries around family, finances or foundation issues. Middle back is not being supported. Neck could be a "pain in the neck", or stiffness could be not flexible on an issue. Shoulders could be you are shouldering a burden. Not standing in your power to allow others to share in responsibility. Taking it all on yourself. "It's all on your shoulders."

So by giving reiki you are allowing this peaceful yet powerful healing energy to flow through you into the recipient to heal and restore their body more fully with life force energy. What people experience is more of a full flow of energy in their physical, mental, and emotional wellbeing. Resulting in a peaceful feeling and relief the following days after a session.

My first ~

I was surprised we got to hands on so quickly. I did not expect to experience what happened next. We respectfully approached our volunteer as we began with Carol's lead of what we had just studied only an hour earlier. I am not exactly sure what I thought I would feel but I immediately felt something flowing magically out of my hands. Like a very steady wave of an energetic current and flow coming down my arms and out my hands pulsing out to the recipient. OMG! One minute I was normal (lol) then next I feel energy pouring out of my hands.

I was able to get eye contact with my friend Becky without disturbing the lady on the table. Becky looked up at me and I mouthed a soundless, WOAHHHHH! She mouthed back, I KNOW! I was in awe observing this beautiful miracle happening and it was an honor to have this energy pulse through me. I had no idea the beauty in my path that was about to unfold from here.

CHAPTER 8

Gifts and Surprises

One of the very first surprises after putting reiki into practice were the images I started to get while giving reiki. I had a client who also loved angels like I did. I thought she may find it interesting what I just learned to do. So while Deb was paying for her haircut at the front desk, she volunteered to let me practice on her. Yay, my first solo session! I wondered would the energy continue for me outside of our class? Was I good enough? My self-doubt came through, but I proceeded anyway and we scheduled a time that week for her to return to my salon after hours.

Deb met me at the salon on a Sunday when we were closed. I brought my boom box (yep, that's how long it's been since I started doing reiki) with a meditation CD I bought to create the relaxing atmosphere to kind of like the music when you get a massage. I explained to Deb to just relax and if anything happens or she has a question just let me know. I followed the steps exactly as Carol taught us.

What happened next I thought I lost my mind. I don't recall being told much around this as a possibility. I bet it would have been funny to have a camera recording my reaction during my first solo session. I always knew I had an active imagination, I thought I was daydreaming at first. I talked to myself when things were happening during the session like … Donna why are you thinking of a tiger right now? Knock it off and focus on reiki. I'd see pictures kind of transparent in front of me. Have you ever heard of the mind's eye? This is where I would see the images.

When I completed the reiki session I let Deb relax quietly for few minutes to come out of her deeply relaxed state. I proceeded to recall step by step the session and record as quickly as I could what chakra (the 7 major the energy centers of the body) I was working on when I received each of the visions.

When Deb was ready I explained to her what I saw in my visions during the session. She asked what it all meant, I said I don't know! I have never experienced anything like this in my life. This is new to me, but it was special for sure. I told her I would look up the images in my books and get back to her. When I called Deb the next day and pieced together the symbolism that I looked up, we found the messages all had a purpose and made total sense. It was like a spiritual scavenger hunt for clues. It all came together in the end.

Invisible Gifts

I will tell you nothing as opened my mind as to the invisible support that exists for us than the gifts the have been shown during reiki sessions. I never expected to have more than me learning about a healing modality. I was simply in essence drawn to it and felt I wanted to help people – and have a tool to care for my kids. It has been such a blessing in connecting more to God than anything I have tried to this point. Like an accelerated path to enlightenment and higher energy, like dipping a toe into the pool of beauty and mysterious realm of Heaven.

I have had loved ones come in with a message for the people I was performing reiki on, I would describe a person to a "T" and their personalities. I would ask does this sound like anyone you know who passed. I would feel an idea of an age of the person I was seeing, I would describe the hair and style of dress. One time someone who passed showed up for a client with a bunny cake, and I described an Aunt feel or grandmother, roller set blondish hair, a very conservative looking older woman in a tweed suit with a skirt. I could feel the bunny cake had something to do with Easter. Apparently it was her Aunt, and Easter was her Aunt's favorite holiday. The bunny cake had a double meaning.…..it was not just symbolizing Easter, it was her aunt telling me she was a good baker. My client laughed and said that's my aunt!

Another time I saw a dog and St. Francis. I often feel ridiculous with what I get in messages, but I have learned I don't need to understand it. I needed to learn to be brave and just communicate what I am getting and for ME not to judge the message. I knew nothing about this person who was a new client who came by referral to me. After I expressed what I received she told me that where she went to college was associated with a Franciscan order of nuns. She then continued to explain there is a statue of St. Francis on campus and the dog I described was her present dog.

I often say to spirit when I get a message, I can't say that they will think I'm crazy. I have learned to say, ok this may sound weird but I saw a statue of St. Francis. Does this mean anything to you? Because that's all I got about St Francis was the statue. Only to find relief when the client connects the dots for me.

Barbara the owner of Bailiwick Hair Center asked me if I would offer to do reiki as a service at the salon when I completed my Master's degree. I was thrilled I could do this at work and was actually added to the computer and on our menu of services at Bailiwick Hair Salon. Hello, I'd like to schedule with Donna for reiki and a haircut. Lol. It was actually in the salon computer as combo service.

I have argued with spirit. How dare it right? I know they love me. And it's a loving banter, I promise. They know my fears and my humor. I trust they know I'm trying, but I am human overcoming early conditioning. The reason for my best growth at Bailiwick Hair center was in learning to trust myself was due to the extraordinary experiences and messages that I received by working on a co-worker and friend who asked me to do reiki on her. Her brother also did reiki so she was very open to it.

Theresa was my one of my best teacher's truly. She really helped me to have confidence in my abilities. Also Spirit began to teach me with their direction during sessions on my clients above and beyond what I learned in my reiki training. Teaching me new ways to remove a persons blocked energy and give it over to the angels. I would listen to their direction and follow their strong promptings. And be given very loving guidance to help my clients in their lives.

Fairies and tribesman, and angels oh my!

Theresa is the kind of girl who I love to be around. She is a fun, sassy, spirited Italian girl. She says what's on her mind in a bold funny way. She intimidated some people, I adore her directness and delivery. She always made me laugh. I began to regularly do reiki on Theresa after I just completed my Master's in Reiki. Meaning I could teach reiki and it's the highest level.

My visions became magnified and the insight I was receiving was incredible. My reiki teacher told me at the Master Level I would be able to zero in on a person's issues. I didn't believe her really. Only because I doubted myself and my ability to do something that was of this magnitude. My dialogue with spirit became easier too. If I didn't understand something I would just ask quietly in my mind while I was doing a session, ok guys what are you trying to tell me?

I put away my reference books as I didn't need them very often anymore. I also learned if I didn't know what something meant that I saw in a session, I would simply observe *where* something was happening. It has relevance in the area I was working on. After the session I would ask my clients if I wasn't clear in a meaning….what does this mean to YOU?

I got fantastic messages with Theresa right off the bat. The fact that she came to me so incredibly open minded, the energy and images would abundantly flow like I never experienced. There was no resistance or walls up trying to protect herself from me or doubt of what I was doing. And she knew my true integrity as a person, so she trusted me completely. The gift to me with Theresa was I learned to truly trust what I was receiving and felt very free to just put out there for her to hear without hesitation no matter how ridiculous it seemed. And let me tell you, it seemed very ridiculous to me!

I'm not telling her THAT!

The most impactful reiki session that stands out of all of Theresa's sessions was right before it was her last day working at Bailiwick where we worked together. I was bummed because she added so much to my day, but she was fulfilling her dream of having her own salon. She specialized in men's hair and was creating a barber shop in her home, and the love of her life Chris had moved in too. So many good things coming together for her.

The biggest lesson for me at this particular session was learning to not assume what a message means when it isn't clear. I saw someone standing in front of me and heard a message that rattled me when I got to Theresa's solar plexus. (Her power center around the stomach area.)

I saw this man with a very stern demeanor, arms crossed, metal rounded glasses, kind of balded and very sparse hair. He was not very tall, wearing plaid trousers and he seemed very smart. He came across like an authority. He grumbled to me almost scolding me, "tell her not to do it!!" I just looked at him. I *assumed* he meant opening the salon. I said in my mind to this man, I can't tell her that. No I won't I said to him! He repeated sternly, "tell her not to do it!"

Well I started to literally break out in a sweat kind of panic, my heart was pounding. That's a huge responsibility on my shoulders, this is her dream. I can't tell her not to do it. He repeated the statement again. I finally said to myself, hold on....maybe there's more to his statement and I am *assuming* the meaning of what he is saying. So I proceeded to ask the man in front of me, tell her not to do what? He said, "tell her not to doubt herself." Well wasn't THAT a lesson for me! *Don't assume. Get clarity*! It was an incomplete thought and statement.

After our session I described the man I saw and what the man said. Theresa said, "that's my dad!" It was a few years later when I was at Theresa's house. She showed me a picture in a shadow box with a pair of barbering shears that she had put together recently. She asked do you know who that is? I looked at the picture and said omg….that's your dad! That's who I saw! It came full circle for me at the moment, that was pretty awesome.

During another reiki session with Theresa I felt all this tiny energy, very low to the ground the entire session. It felt light and dancey. Fluttering around. This was entirely different than any reiki session ever. I always was excited to compare our notes from our sessions afterwards. Because I never knew what I was about it experience with my friend. It was something completely different every time!

I described how I felt low to the ground energy, very tiny little energies, and earthy. Her description of her experience was very much the same as mine. I finally just said, "Theresa I didn't believe in fairies, but I think they are showing me they exist." She said that surprised her since I was so open minded. Apparently it was time to be opened a bit more.

Another time Theresa scheduled a session with me prior to her wedding. Immediately I got a very primal old group of wise men gathering in her honor. Like a tribal or Native American kind of feel. About half way through the session I saw a red fox then it shifted into a white fox. She just looked at me a little taken back when I was describing what I saw. She told me she was deciding between two different outfits to wear as the bride, one had a red fox fur collar the other had a white fox fur collar. Her wedding was in the cooler time of year around Thanksgiving and she an outside ceremony, she was such a beautiful bride!

Another time I saw Archangel Raphael larger than life, who is the archangel of healing. He had very big wings that spread wide filling the wall of facial room standing at the bottom of her feet. I could feel him enhancing the healing during the session as if the entire room emanated a special light. Just quiet, no words, just feeling his huge magnificence and healing Theresa. I was in awe at the vision only feet in front of me. At the end Theresa told me she kept seeing green. I loved this feedback! Archangel Raphael's energy color is GREEN!

All of these sessions with her being so incredibly open to energy work and trusting me, she helped me to be free to receive messages and connect better than I ever had with anyone. I now felt so free to practice verbalizing what I was receiving. I learned if I didn't understand something, to direct my questions to spirit or to my client. To trust what I was getting and how the energy shows up is perfect. All of this prepared me for the most important reiki session of my life.

CHAPTER 9

Advanced Universal Energy

Learning how to read energy, ask questions, and patiently await for the Universe to respond in ways that are meaningful to you is really a fun way to live. What a great feeling to be tapped into this invisible world of spirit. To know that the Divine is so easily accessible and understood with practice. This became my world, and I was never so grateful to my life path that led me to understand this language from Heaven than in the following story. Heaven or the Light is here to help us really when we ask, but there are times God lovingly answers before we even call on Him.

The next two stories I was fortunate for God to anticipate my needs, and what is of the greatest gift to me. I never asked. He knew my needs and lovingly helped prepare me. I was at a level in my awareness where I allowed myself to completely and openly give my heart to God, Jesus, the Holy Spirit, the angels and fully expect them to talk to me in the now everyday all day. Thank God for this two way street to not only ask, but also in honing my ability to hear and notice the ways the invisible realm speaks to us.

It's mom's time

Have you ever dreaded as a little kid irrationally losing your mom or your special person whoever that person may be? I remember having the realization for the first time in first grade that my mom under no uncertain terms would absolutely die. No avoiding it, everyone is going to die.

My mom was sickly from about 50 years old onward and upward. She escaped death many times, having superior doctors at Hershey Medical Center in Hershey, Pennsylvania. The laundry list of disorders were Cushing's Disease, almost having to have her legs amputated due to poor circulation, leg bypass, a kidney bypass, heart disease, heart attacks, stints, high blood pressure and more. On so many meds, many surgeries, I have said mom was like a cat with 9 lives. There were a couple of times the doctors said you better get here to see your mother, she may not make it.

In 2007 we got the news my mom needed open heart surgery and was going to get a valve replacement. I told my mom, I am not getting a good feeling about this surgery mom I don't think you should do it. You know I have never told you not to do something. I was never concerned before, but this time it is a different feeling of it's not going to go well. I kept repeating, I don't think you should do this. My mom always trusted her doctor's advice 100%, after all they were best doctors around.

Before the surgery they did the usual pre-op testing. My mom called to tell me the tests showed spots on her lungs and lymph nodes. I may have neglected to tell you my mom was an avid smoker for 30 years. About 2 packs a day. At this stage of the game I was 40 years old and already have lost several friends due to cancer. I understand that when you open someone up surgically, the cancer has the potential to metastasize.

Without hesitation I said to my mom, what if the worst case is cancer? Shouldn't we address that first? See how far the cancer is if that's the case. Why put your body through open heart surgery and valve replacement if you are terminally ill? Wouldn't you rather live out your days without putting yourself through such a major surgery? Shouldn't we be clear before you proceed with the heart surgery?

The doctors told my mom she would need a strong heart to handle if it is cancer. I 100% disagreed with my entire being shouting PLEASE don't do this. However, you can't tell a doctor you have a strong hunch, and I am an intuitive hairdresser and I just know.

My mom was on the operating table for 11 hours. It was supposed to be a 5 hour surgery. My niece's friend was a doctor in the OR told my her that my mom's heart began to crumble in the surgeon's hands from so many heart attacks. My mom proceeded to have a heart attack on the operating table during the surgery, and also the next day.

She struggled over the next few months, spending most of her time in bed very weak. Breathing was becoming more an issue, and the oxygen tank was always with my mom when we left the house, and it was always kept by her chair. We were all very concerned. Mom even told me not to come home for Easter, she wasn't going to church or having the family dinner. Woah! No family gathering or church? My worry grew deeper.

My mom decided about a month later she wanted to celebrate my sister Deb's 50th birthday in mid-August with a party. Which I kind of thought was odd since my sister's birthday was October 19th. Family was everything to my mom. She would spend weeks making sure all the details and planning were perfect for our get togethers. My sister's birthday was no exception.

Deb had a fabulous party at Town Perk, in Bloomsburg Pennsylvania. My parents favorite place was filled with many of my sisters friends from high school, college and our extended family. I could see my mom forcing a smile and toughing it out the whole weekend. Spending much of her time in her chair at home, oxygen draped under her nose, not smiling and not talking much. Just breathing was an effort, and talking stole the little oxygen she was getting. It was very hard to watch my mom struggle and not experience joy with us as she so loved to do.

The morning after the party I saw my mom reclined in her favorite chair with her oxygen. I asked her if she wanted me to give her a little reiki. She said, "oh, I don't want to be a bother." I said, "you are my mom, believe me it's no bother!" She agreed, and so I began to give my mom reiki beginning at the top of her head at the crown chakra. I wasn't feeling anything as I normally do, no energy, no warmth, no pulsing. Normally when I place my hands on someone the energy just begins to flow through me automatically. Especially since receiving my Master level, energy just pours out of my hands like a waterfall, and now I felt nothing?

I blamed myself for not connecting and surely I must be doing something wrong. I moved my hands to my mom's throat area and it was same thing, nothing. Heart nothing. Finally when I got to my mom's belly I started to feel energy. I was like oh THERE it is, I got it now. At first I tried to make sense from a mental understanding and said to myself maybe I couldn't feel the energy because I was tired or maybe slightly hungover from the party. So as I continued to work on her solar plexus I saw something I had never experienced or heard about. I just watched with curiosity at the unfolding in front of me.

I saw a white energy gathering like a pool above me with a white trail coming from the bottom of my mom's feet. It looked like my mom's spirit leaving her body through the bottom of her feet and going upwards to the ceiling and gathering to the energy above us. I watched this energy rising as mom was laying back in her favorite recliner. I remember thinking, OMG I think she has started the ascension process.

In reiki I sense a person's energy field or soul. I started to understand why I felt nothing at my mom's head and heart, because what I saw was no life force at her head or her heart. I was calmer than I thought being given this life altering information and wondered if what I was feeling was accurate. I also understood this is really a very loving piece of information to give to me and they (Spirit) are showing me something pretty big. Because if this is the case, they just gave me a clue to make sure I live with no regrets, seize this moment with great care to show love to my mom more than I ever have.

As I moved down to my mom's legs which is where she had circulation problems for years, it felt like jello was clinging to my hands that I could not get off. It seemed to energetically accumulate up my arms. So I instinctively felt to pull out the energetic goop from my mom's leg area. Sluggish, sticky energy that I felt I needed to remove it from my arms and hands after I removed it from my mom. This was a new sensation for me as well. I felt as if removing this clingy sludgy energy was going to help my mom transition when it was her time, freeing her in a sense.

By the end of our session my mom was feeling much better and was able to actually take off the oxygen. She was breathing much easier and she had been restored energy enough to get up and walk around and seemed more like herself. She was again able to enjoy a conversation with ease.

There was a time my mom thought reiki was not of God. Even though my mom in the past said ok to receiving reiki at her hospital bedside, she would almost pull away from me. I realized previously my mom was letting me give her reiki because she loved me, but she was afraid of it. I had said one time, mom I can tell you are uncomfortable so I am going to stop. She had told me ok. But since that time, she has had reiki done by a family nun who also teaches others reiki. And mom also questioned her priest around his thoughts of reiki. Father told my mom he believes reiki is of God.

So what she said to me next was so meaningful to me. I think my mom knew as I did too, this was our goodbye. I thought to myself, I better tell my mom everything I ever have wanted to tell her. I think this is could be my last time face to face with my mom. I recognized spirit was giving me an opportunity to have the most important moment of my life. Telling my mom of my gratitude and appreciation for all she was to me. Everything I would want my mom to know before leaving this life I understood now is the moment to speak what I need to say.

I told my mom how blessed I was to have her as my mother, and she showed me how to be love in the world, and important it is to have a relationship with God. She showed me how important family is. How incredibly grateful I was for her to teach me all she did in life and how much I deeply loved her. Many more heartfelt personal sharings with us holding hand to hand, toe to toe, heart to heart.

My mom told me 3 things that day that meant the world to me. She told me I have such a gift with my reiki, how it *is* of God and I'm a gift to so many. The other was that I was such a good mother and am so good to my girls. And what good girls I have and it was because of me. The last gift she

71

told me was that I did the right thing by leaving my husband. There was a time my parents didn't stand by me in leaving. Catholics don't believe in divorce.

I was so happy to know where my mom stood presently. For years she had disapproved some of my choices. She has evolved in her perceptions on the topics that were very important to me. She now appreciated and supported me for being authentic to myself. I left later that Sunday back to Reading, PA. This day was the last time I ever saw my mother alive.

The following week my mom was having some serious issues with her breathing. I told my mom on the phone, please don't delay in getting to the hospital if you need to go. It's not like a broken finger you can live with, you need air to breathe. My mom promised me she would go to the ER if she needed. The next morning at 6 a.m. my phone was ringing with my mom's ring tone. I knew before I answered the call the moment was here. It was the moment I dreaded my whole life.

It's in the Heart

This next story isn't about a reiki session. But rather to express what I learned so much because of this beautiful and generous Universal Life Force Energy. How we are all one even after death, our connection and love continues. That our loved ones come to see us as they did for my clients during their reiki sessions. More was possible than I ever was taught growing up. How when you live in awareness and alignment you open yourself to recognizing so much more communication than you would ever imagine in your own special divine relationship.

I have learned to recognize when mysterious happenings come about to not to brush them off as coincidence. My opening to this energy and years of study enabled me to receive and understand messages from spirit and my newly passed over mother almost immediately. I am certain we all receive these messages, but most of us can go through life unconscious, unaware to what is being communicated to us. The purpose of me sharing all of these stories is to share with you the possibilities beyond our two dimensional world as you know it. Remember early on I was scared, misinformed, and often a skeptic to these kinds of happenings. Anything is possible friends.

Within minutes of my mom passing I said loudly, "ok Mom, I need to see you somehow." "Please let me know you are ok." "Please reach out and communicate to me, I know you can!" "Ask God and the angels to help you reach me." "I really need to hear from you, please."

I of course wasn't this calm initially. Upon hearing the news, I dropped to the floor and sobbed uncontrollably a gut-wrenching cry for several minutes. Having a 6 and a 12 year old, I needed to pull it together for them. There they stood over me looking so bewildered not knowing how to handle what was happening. Watching the person they count on 24/7 fall to pieces momentarily. I went to my downstairs powder room to splash cold water on my face before getting my girls some breakfast.

I peeked through my blurred vision from crying and saw a red mark around my collar bone in the mirror. I looked closer and it was in the shape a heart. I thought oh great, I am breaking out in hives for the funeral.

I tried to wash it off thinking it was makeup, I saw no other red marks anywhere else on my body. I walked up to my girls and asked, "hey what does this look like to you guys?" Jadin said, "Oh, where did you get the heart tattoo mommy I want one!" Ok, so validated on the shape! I thought wow, maybe it's a symbol from my mom that she loves me and is with me. After all I had asked for a sign only minutes before.

We got packed up rather quickly and were on our way for several days to help plan the funeral and to support each other as a family. On the way all I could think about was I can't wait to get something of my mom's and put it on me. I needed my mom close to me in any way possible in the physical. I longed to feel a bit of my mom near me.

Previously my mom told all of us what we would be getting after she passed. Her wishes were spelled out with meticulously detailed instructions and were stored in her grey metal lock box. Mom would show us repeatedly throughout the years where the metal box was in her closet. I always walked away from the conversation when my mom started with, "When I die, this is where I keep the box." I figured I am one of 5 kids let someone else handle this conversation. I would get weak in the knees and my insides start to crumble at the very thought of losing my mom.

The 3 girls in my family were each getting a carat of diamonds. I couldn't remember who was getting which diamond. I thought I was getting the marquise solitaire, which I believe was a 40th anniversary present from my dad. There was a carat cocktail ring, and also my grandmother's half carat engagement ring, and my mom's half carat engagement ring as a total of 1 carat. I really was hoping for my mom and grams ring. About 95 years of marriage between them. And my mom wore them everyday. I so wanted a good marriage someday. For me to have their rings symbolized one of my dreams of a better marriage. Plus they were two of the most special women to ever touch my life. To have something so treasured of theirs on me always sounded so comforting.

I arrived home and we all took the time to comfort each other sharing the loss of our mom. For my dad it was his other half and true love for 60 years. I noticed the gathering of photos already on our dining room table with beautiful memoirs that were beginning to be assembled. We started going through the very old pictures, it was actually fun uncovering new bits of info we never knew about our mom as we began to dig through her scrapbooks and boxes.

After a while, I asked about the rings. I was told by my brother Mike that mom's jewelry was missing. My heart sunk with the news. My brother and dad driven to the hospital to go get my mom's jewelry and the hospital staff said she never had jewelry on. Let me tell you, my mom NEVER took off her jewelry....ever! Well so many scenarios being tossed trying to solve this mystery. I went to go look in my mom and dad's bedroom and was told by my family they already looked all through the entire room. It's not in there.

I managed to get myself calm and asked my mom where is it, I heard "it's in the house." I went to my mom's room and started looking in the logical place, her jewelry armoire. No success finding anything. So next I sat on her bed just wanting to see if I could connect with her on a spiritual level, so I meditated. I prayed and asked for help to find my mom's jewelry, I wanted to feel her close to me in any way. I had trouble meditating as of course, I just lost my mom hours prior. Now I am in her bedroom where she collapsed and the ambulance crew were working on her less than 24 hours before.

Suddenly I felt so inspired to just get up and look around. Just connect to mom in any way you can and forget about the jewelry. As I stood, I felt pulled like a magnet to her clothes armoire. I was wondering what was her life like in the last few days as I gazed through the contents. She had moved her sweatshirts into the armoire, that was new. I wondered when she made that change and started to pick up shirts and smell them. Her whole armoire smelled like Calvin Klein Eternity.

I mindlessly followed wherever my heart led me in those moments forgetting I was on a mission, now I was just thinking of my mom and wanting to be close to her. Next I opened a drawer and noticed a Longaberger basket I had never seen. It was in an odd location for my mom to store this with her clothes tucked out of the way. I pulled out the 5 inch or so basket in the shape of a heart.

I paused just staring for a second kind of immobilized asking myself, could it be?

Suddenly I recalled the heart on my collar bone wondering what exactly my mom was saying showing me a heart on my body that remained for hours. Is this wishful thinking? I carefully opened the heart basket looking through the contents. I saw some very sparkly objects in that heart, it was filled with diamonds and gold. Everything looked very different kind of rolling around loosely when it wasn't on my mom, but just laying there was everything we were looking for. YES!

There it was, all my mom's jewelry that she wore everyday and never took off. Rings included in that heart basket hidden in an odd spot. My mom must have known it was her time, and put her jewelry away for safekeeping.

My mom also made a list that last day for my dad of my brothers and sisters phone numbers and mine as well. Mom showed my dad the list by the phone, "here are all of the kids numbers if anything happens to me." My mom was organized and still cared for her family even in her final moments. And she listened to her intuition in her final moments, she knew and tucked away her valuables for safekeeping.

I ran out to the dining room where my family was still around the table. I burst out saying, "I found mom's jewelry!" They asked where did you find it, we looked everywhere! How did you find it? I said, "I prayed, then I listened." My brother Rick chuckled, paused then repeated with a big smile said, "you prayed, then you listened." He kept looking at me his eyes gleaming with his ear to ear smile. I said, remember my heart pointing to my collarbone, that's what mom was telling me hours ago. *It's in the heart.*

More to the Message ~ It's in the Heart

Looking back now, that statement that was given to me that day from my mom in spirit form has an even truer meaning of life for me. That statement is packed with such wisdom that I would come to know a few years later when I studied with Louise Laffey and the Wish teachings. Which is New Heart Movement Teachings.

It's in the heart, all of the answers and guidance. It is the center of where Divine Intelligence and the physical plane intersect. Where we are best served to make all of our decisions and connect to our truth. The heart center guides us, it tells us when we are out of alignment and also we can recognize when we are in alignment.

It pounds when we are nervous, letting us know this is not safe, or when we out of alignment in our thoughts. When we are on the right path our heart feels fulfilled, sometimes like it's bursting with joy or that YES feeling. When we are in full flow, at one with the Divine you can feel the ease and grace. When things don't flow, we most likely are allowing our fears or distractions to take over. All we have to do to get back in flow is just be focused with in our heart and breathe. We can shift in literally seconds to our heart simply by focusing our attention there and just being in the present moment. Away from regret about the past or worry about the future. Heart presence is a powerful place to be.

CHAPTER 10

Ask and it is Given

This statement my friends I have lived and learned to be true. But the key to the wisdom here is to think of *asking* as the activator. Like putting your intention in motion. Next we let go in faith with no need to concern ourselves the how's and the when the wisdom or answers will present themselves. I am sure you can think of examples that you have had in your lifetime where you have prayed with such conviction, yet stood waiting with anticipation to hear any answers and maybe it took a very long time. Can you think of other times where have you had something that seemed to be answered almost immediately after asking?

It seems as though the issues that are so very important to you and close to your heart could keep you waiting what seems like forever. Why is that? And conversely many requests you nonchalantly ask for such as, boy I sure would like "that".... and it shows as if my a magic delivery service. Of course I believe in the higher order and the wisdom of God's timing. However, I also believe we often can keep things just outside of our grasp by not having faith or aligning with the natural flow by being in trust in the ways of the Divine.

I can't tell you how many times I have been unattached just making a verbal statement such as, I sure am hungry Spirit. I could go for a cupcake can you send me some food please? I would be double booked with clients all day at work and wouldn't have an opportunity to make a food run. Kind of joking but definitely putting my request out there. Often I wished to have a Starbucks coffee please. Next thing I know a client walks in with a Starbucks latte for me, or a basket full of freshly baked muffins made for just for me by my client that day. I have so many manifestation stories and signs that I regularly receive the topic could span books and books.

The biggest lesson I have observed is that if we remain unattached; meaning not giving it a second thought, putting our prayers or requests out there and trusting it is in God's hands by not obsessing or worrying about trying to control it....your desires can show up much easier. Just keep going on with your life and have fun not wondering is it on its way yet? Where could it possibly be?

This is where I find getting heart centered and surrendering to God in trust and faith is the best to live a miraculous life. (Being in flow or non-resistance.) The more we are attached to an outcome, the more that energy seems to keep what we are hoping for from us.

Actually in truth we are keeping what we want from us more accurately by doubting and worrying (thinking about not having it, or not having faith) which causes resistance to the natural flow of energy and the very thing that we want. The magic and miracles make such an impact for me when the timing and delivery appear at just the perfect time after I literally have forgotten and have let it go.

Remember .....*like attract likes in Universe.* So worry and fear, you will get more to worry and be fearful about. Joy attracts more joy. Love attracts more to love. Good high vibration energy attracts more good high vibration energy. The Universal Matrix moves the players and the attraction of people and situations into your experience according to your vibration and beliefs. Change your focus and the trajectory of what you had been thinking can suddenly realign you into a more desirable flow instantly. Meaning, if your beliefs are that you doubt it can ever happen, then most likely that is keeping you in resistance to you hopes. If you surrender and keep the faith....the energy flows a gorgeous full flow.

I hope you enjoy my stories of my experience to drive the "how" I asked and the miracles big and small that were delivered in entertaining ways to me. But you set things in motion with your energy, your focus and by asking. But letting go and faith are a big part of the equation as well. And I also learned in this next story how putting God and our relationship is number one.

Soldraham and my precious gift

I still hold this experience as one of the most miraculous experiences of my lifetime. At this stage my life was in pretty good place. My husband had started making pretty good money, things were well with my business, Morgan was easier as she was 4 years old now. We lived in a super neighborhood we all loved which brought us much fun and great friendships.

My mom had another one of her scary moments that she pulled on one of her 9 lives she seemed to have. As I sat worried about my mom at Hershey Medical Center in the waiting room with my siblings, I had the thought Morgan can't be alone. What would I do without my siblings? We are all there for each other in times of crisis. Coming to the hospital from far and wide to be by mom's side, all at our best with love for each other in times like this. We offered each other humor, wisdom, and comfort in our togetherness. I left the hospital strongly feeling Morgan needs a brother or sister to go through life with, someone who can share special times even after I am gone.

My husband was on board for this venture and so we went down the path of trying to get pregnant. I was approaching a year of trying and no luck. I worried what if this took several years and I have issues to work through? I called my OB/GYN and they agreed I should be tested. I made an appointment and I was booked in September with a fertility specialist.

I had been praying of course for help to conceive. Was I not hitting the right timing? Were we trying too hard? I read all the books on optimal timing, frequency, but was disappointed month after month after month. I tried the ovulation tests which looked like I *never* ovulated. My mom had given me her tiny little prayer book to the Blessed Mother. She thought it would help me in my quest for a baby.

The pages were very tattered and you could tell it had comforted my mom many a day on her life's journey as a woman and mother. The book was given to my mom by my Irish Catholic grandmother many years ago. I kept looking outside of me for answers, my mind was consumed on one topic. Baby, baby, baby. Force, force, force. My control, what can "I" do. Do, do, do!

Until one day, it all became clear and knocked me on my butt because Heaven touched me in a way that would change my life forever. I learned from this moment what can happen if we are open and aware to receiving help in ways we had never told was ok or possible when I sat in catholic school.

Step 1 ~ Be One with God

I began to meditate one day as I often did. I was in my favorite room in my house, with cathedral ceilings and surrounded by huge windows. Enjoying the gorgeous sunlight that filled the room, I could feel the sun's warmth on my skin. I was pretty good meditating by now and could get deep quickly by this point.

My meditation music was playing, I felt peaceful and very relaxed when all of a sudden I felt this BIG presence right there in front of me. I mean humongously BIG! It felt different than ever in my experience of angels and energy. I was so incredibly terrified. I jumped up and said, NO WAY, you are not coming here! I assumed it was negative energy because it was so intense and felt like it spanned a big portion of the space in front of me.

Then something told me gently.....just check the energy. Just check it, I heard a soft nurturing prompting again. Still kind of shaken, I asked are you of light, are you of Jesus? If you are not of the light you HAVE TO GO! You must be of Jesus!

The energy stayed with me unwaveringly. That signaled to me it was of the Light. It was of God. I was told that is the Universal Law by Nancy years ago. This is how you protect yourself. God is the highest power. If you call in God and tell an energy to go if it is not of the Light and Love of God, it has to go, command it. The Light always wins and has the Highest Power. Universal law.

I felt an inner prompting to go upstairs to my bedroom and to grab paper to do an angel writing. Slightly afraid but now curious. I could feel Spirit urging me to keep going. When I say Spirit, it could be God, Jesus the angels, Holy Spirit or an Ascended Master. I can feel when it's Divine.

So I grabbed some paper and pen, I got relaxed as much as I could and looked in front of me. As I tuned into the energy I could feel it at the foot of my bed. I proceeded to ask the force in front of me who are you? Why are you here? Over the next few minutes, the answer was revealed and a miracle resulted from this powerful visitor.

I was told......

> *"I am Soldraham, a powerful force of the Light. I am very close to the vibration of God, the reason you fear me is you have not experienced a scope of this magnitude. Your child will take heed in the womb at your request when you become One with God. It will be in HIS timing, not yours. Be one with God."*

I have to tell you the voice that came was booming, kind of like the God's voice to Moses in the movie the Ten Commandments. It was deep and deliberate like James Earl Jones, and felt all knowing. I didn't question it, it was authoritative, not wordy. Just facts and done. Clear, deep and purposeful. Not soft or angelic which is what I normally experienced. I felt it wasn't bad like I initially feared when I felt the energy before.

I now understand I was afraid because it was quite immense and powerful. I never have heard of Soldraham. But do we know *everything* about the invisible realm of God as humans? No matter how much experience, training or degrees we have it's speculation, or passed down information that we take as written in stone at times or limited to certain authorities.

82

We would be foolish to think we have the corner on understanding all there is to know about God and the workings of the Universe.

And then there were cherubs

More to this story unfolding, when Soldraham completed his message, *the energy changed.* I went from experiencing this HUGE force in that was at the foot of my bed to immediately shifting to a different place and different energy altogether. The focus went from that big energy of Soldraham that felt about 10 feet away to now being super close.

I noticed the sweetest most loving energy. I just watched as the little cherubs as they swirled around my vision in front of me. The feeling went from being of a great magnitude, to now a very soft and beautifully comforting energy. Seeing the little baby like angels, I could get lost in their sweetness. Next thing I was hearing words again but in a much softer voice. I grabbed the pen and started to take dictation like a banshee again right underneath of Soldraham's message. The words came so quickly I could not comprehend what I was writing. Then the writing completely and suddenly stopped.

Soldraham was gone, the cherub like little angels were gone. I sat for a second taking in what just happened. I looked down at the page holding it in front of me curious to see what they said. This is what I read that came from my own hand, pen to page, yet I had no idea what I about to read.

> *"Hail Mary Mother of God, bestow upon me a child whom all good things come. Beseech my prayer and bless the path of my intended for he shall bear witness the sound of God."*

I studied the paper in my hands, still kind of in awe and processing. OMG, I think I was just dictated a prayer! I sat a moment reflecting on the words written in front of me, I believe I was just given a gift to help me conceive. There was no directions, but as I experienced in my life many times I had a deep *knowing,* I just knew what to do.

I realized I was making the idea of a baby my focus 24/7, obsessed really. According to Soldraham, I wasn't putting my relationship with God first and putting myself in HIS care. So in that moment I decided, ok I am making God my focus and our relationship in every moment and letting go my tight grip. Soldraham told me I would get pregnant when I was one with God. From this moment forward I tuned into the omnipresent force consciously in my body, my mind and my soul. Feeling into the oneness whenever I remembered.

So I went from an IF I can get pregnant, to feeling ok I was just told in the most magnificent way I need to focus on being one with God and follow these directions. Oneness with pure love and light. *I had lost sight of God in all of this baby making journey.* I had been going into the worry all day long with thoughts of maybe I can't get pregnant becoming my fear and focus.

I said my prayer to the Blessed Mother that the angels dictated to me every time I thought of it. I went from reading it off of an index card to being able to let it roll off my tongue. When I was riding in the car, between clients, standing in line at the grocery store waiting to pay for my groceries I would remember to feel the oneness, the love and presence of God.

I had scheduled a visit to see my sister Deb before the summer ended. She lived about 10 minutes away from Ocean City, New Jersey. Morgan and I were looking forward to visiting my sister for our special girls' weekend. Deb asked if it was ok for her boyfriend to come and hang out with us for a bit. She explained I may have fun chatting with Bill, as his hobby was reflexology. Deb knew I liked holistic and spiritual kinds of things. I said oh, very cool and what a coincidence! I just happened to recently take a reflexology class.

Bill and I shared many philosophies, he had a great sense of humor and was very down to earth. After spending the afternoon chatting he finally said give me your foot, would you like a reflexology treatment? I said sure, I never actually had a treatment for myself.

I swung my foot around to Bill and he started pressing around my ankle, it kind of hurt. He zeroed in on something. He said, "do you know you have a pea sized lump right here?" Neither one of us knew what point this coordinated within the body. I ran upstairs and pulled from my suitcase my reflexology book and looked up that area where the lump was located. It was truly like a small pea, usually it feels like a grain of sand under the skin. I was taught it's a calcium deposit under the skin if there is something you need to break up in your system. Well lo and behold, the location of the lump was in the reproductive system.

He knew I was trying to get pregnant and advised me to work on breaking that up and drink lots of water to flush it out of my system. So I worked on the spot for the next few days, and then I scheduled a full reflexology appointment with my reiki teacher who did many modalities of healing. By the time I saw Carol, she said I don't feel anything now. She was right, I felt my ankle and it was gone. I had worked it out!

It didn't take long, the prayers to the Blessed Mother, aligning and focusing on my oneness with God. It was by no coincidence being led to my sister's boyfriend showing me where I held the blockage in my body….within 2 weeks I was pregnant. I called the fertility Dr. to say I was going to cancel my appointment, of course they asked why. I told them I was pregnant! The nurse laughed and said well that's the best reason!

I almost left my sister a message on her answering machine to be funny, ummmm your boyfriend got me pregnant! I didn't, because you never know who is there when she listens. Keep in mind this was a time when everyone in the room heard the messages left on your answering machine. I couldn't wait to tell Deb my news. I have been so blessed, and yes, I shifted my focus to God. Jadin's middle name is Mary, as I know the Blessed Mother played a beautiful role in bringing me my girl. My prayers were heard. Hence Jadin's name, which means "God has heard."

Big takeaway for me here. God and your relationship is always first. Always. Give thanks, give praise, and give him your concerns. My client Charles used to say, "Put it at the foot of the cross". I asked him, what do you mean? He pulled out a construction nail from his pocket, he carried it with him always to remind himself daily to lay his concerns at Jesus's feet at the foot of the cross and leave it there. He said, "don't pick your problem back up, you gave it to Him. It's God's.

Charles advice was given with such heartfelt grace in his delivery, it was so helpful in me getting my mind around truly surrendering. Why would we want to take it back he said to me. One time as I was so tightly holding onto the way something needed to play out, insisting on my way which led me to struggle. My reiki teacher Carol brought up my need to surrender my situation. I said, "but I want to be in charge of my life." She said, *how's that working for you?* I broke out into roaring laughter. She was 100% right.

I came upon this impactful message of oneness in a miraculous way. *I did ask for help*, but *my worrying wasn't allowing me the oneness with God.* I had been at one with worry, not at oneness with God. When I interfered with the if's and how's, tried to handle things by myself, I was shown in a powerful way how to honor God and it would fall into place.

The Wish Training ~ Asking and letting go of the how's

I had been giving reiki at work and to friends for a few years. Started to do a little bit of readings for people who witnessed me having some pretty wild things happen and wanted me to try it for them. I really loved helping people find inner peace and sharing what I have learned. To teach them that they can influence what shows up for them by managing their energy in where they put their focus and bringing people back to their God connection.

Remember Theresa? My co-worker who I gave reiki to? The little Italian dynamo! Well I was completely honored and humbled when she said she wanted to learn reiki and she didn't want to ask anyone but me to be her teacher. So I taught the first section of the reiki class one Friday. We had a really cool experience during the attunement, I received lots of visions I shared with Theresa afterwards. One of the visions I saw was an angel over Theresa with his arms open like a "Y" above his head. I felt strongly it was Archangel Metatron, I need to look him up to see why he came and what he symbolized because I knew nothing about him.

We were going to skip Saturday and continue our class on Sunday, as there was a really big holistic conference about an hour away. I was excited because Doreen Virtue was going to be teaching and available for a meet and greet. I have read so many of her books and often use her cards for readings.

The entire purpose for me to go to this event was to meet Doreen, hug her and tell her of how grateful I was for her. Her books and cards helped me hone my gifts and trust myself in what I was receiving. I wanted to say thank you in person.

I was pleasantly surprised when I ran into a friend at the expo I had met my Charles Virtue training a couple years prior. Her name is Judy Toma, she is an angel practitioner, producer and actress. We both feel there was no accident of us crossing paths, we totally enjoy each other.

About 30 minutes after our hello's at the expo, Judy ran up to me carrying about 4 royal blue shiny boxes. She very enthusiastically encouraged me to check out the Wish booth. "Donna go down this aisle you *have* to play this game called *THE WISH™*." She went on to explain it's amazing and she just bought four games for a retreat she was hosting.

I said to myself well if Judy says it's worth checking out it must be good. I found the booth that I passed and ignored multiple times. I feel like spirit was saying excuse me....if you aren't going to pay attention we are sending reinforcements to guide you there.

So I was greeted by Jessica who sat my then boyfriend Brad and I down and explained the game to us. What is your greatest wish we were asked? We were told THE WISH™ game is designed to help you release what may be blocking you to receiving your greatest wish. It helps you understand how you have been thinking which may influence what you attract. The game is played around an infinity symbol which representing NO LIMITS. As you move throughout the game, clues are revealed to help you discover what beliefs you are holding that you may not even be in your awareness. You could be unconsciously standing in your own way of shaping your goals and dreams into reality.

So I wrote out my wish and played with a man I never met before who was sitting next to me. Interesting thing is when you play the Wish™ with people, they can offer their perspectives which could be ideas that may not have crossed your mind. Also, common threads often appear between the players I was informed.

The man's name who played with me was Richard. I said, "oh my dad's name is Richard." He shared with me that his wife was battling adrenal cancer, which is rare. I extended my compassion for his situation and their experience. I recognized another connection of us sharing the game together. My mom had a rare disease of her adrenals called cushing's disease and struggled with her health for quite some time due to effects of her adrenals. There were many interesting commonalities between Richard and myself throughout the game and the wisdom that unfolded in that short span of time was enough for me to recognize - this was a powerful tool.

The game is used by counselors, coaches, psychologists, and also in corporate to help with goal setting. THE WISH™ had regularly been played at the Deepak Chopra Center as well. I expressed to Brad I really think I can help people with this. Brad saw my excitement and said he would buy it for me as an early Christmas present. I smiled and asked, "but you are Jewish do you do that, buy Christmas presents?" He laughed and said yes. I was very grateful for Brad's generosity and said thank you. Next thing I know Jessica said we want to take your picture with Louise the creator of The Wish. I said sure, ok!

I had no idea who Louise was. She was this beamingly gorgeous petite woman with a wonderful Australian accent. Louise very graciously chatted with me for a few minutes. I told her how much I enjoyed the game, she then proceeded to ask me if I wanted to come to the training to learn how to properly facilitate. I said, "oh yes I would love to learn how to do this in the most beneficial way." So I asked Louise when is the training? She said, SATURDAY! (it was exactly a week away and the training lasting a total of 5 days.) Then I asked where it was, Louise said FLORIDA. OMG.

I'd need a flight, a hotel and it was exactly a week away, and it was about $1200 for the class.

In my mind I tried to hold it together and be polite. That was an absurd thought! I told Louise thank you, but I am a single mom, I am totally booked with clients at work for weeks, I don't know who I'd get to watch my girls, blah, blah, blah. Negative Nelly I was. Louise just smirked and said, ok here's my number if you change your mind and walked away. Louise didn't push at all, but had a look in her eyes of "ok we will let you come to the conclusion yourself".

So on the way home I couldn't help but replay my conversation with Louise. I laughed at myself while driving, ok really Donna? You just told the creator of the wish *all* of the limits you have, childcare, work, and money. And the game is about NO LIMITS and you just spilled out to the creator of this game all of yours.

About 15 minutes into my drive I began to have a serious conversation with God. Listen, I feel like you are telling me this is really important. I am asking for your help in getting there because I feel like if I take money from my account I could hurt my family in the end. So much mommy guilt and full of I can'ts. If you want me to go, and if I can help people with this game as a tool, and it would change my life for the better and other people's lives being of service for You, please I am asking for You to send me the money BEFORE I need it. And I also ask that it happens within a few days and all the details fall into place. Clients, childcare etc. If it doesn't come, I will know you don't want me to go. And I truly let it go.

The following day I had the second day of training for Theresa's Level 1 Reiki at her house. I brought the game with me, to share with Theresa. I thought she would think it's cool. A little bit later in the day, Theresa said to me. How many levels of reiki are there? I said three. She said to me, I really like what you have taught me so far so I would like to take all three levels with you. How about if I prepay you and you can have the money now so you can go to your training. I just looked at Theresa stunned and said, I can't do that. She said why? I replied," I would feel badly". She said to me, "you have trouble letting people help you." "You need to sit around that." Lol, one the things as I said that I love Theresa is her directness. She called me out and she was absolutely correct.

Long story short, I had the money to attend the training the very next day after I asked God to help me. The details fell into place with ease in with who would watch my girls, and my clients willingly and happily rebooked. I was concerned my two daughters would be upset I was leaving and think I was selfish for spending money on myself. Their response was mommy you should go, you never do anything for yourself. I had their blessing. I was guilt free and was about to embark on a knowledge that would permanently change how I navigate life. My understanding of energy would grow beyond any teachings I have ever experienced. Again, Ask and you shall receive. And just how everything is connected with people, events, and timings.

An little extra tidbit

Speaking of connections, remember when I had done Theresa's attunement that I mentioned earlier in the chapter, and I had seen Archangel Metatron in a vision over Theresa's head? I really didn't know much about AA Metatron, just that he existed. I looked him up when I got home that night. I read not only does he help people how to use their spiritual power for good, but he is also associated with sacred geometry.

At my Wish training which was a week after I had the vision with Theresa, I realized why I saw Archangel Metatron during the attunement. I learned there is so much sacred geometry in THE WISH™ throughout the design, symbolism and energy of the game. Little did I know I was about to learn a bit about sacred geometry in THE WISH™ numerology and energy associated with each number.

The Tumbling Trampoline

This story is a bit more light hearted about asking and receiving. A little less miraculous and life changing as the last two. But this experience really impacted me by observing again how when we are unattached to an outcome, we attract things with ease.

It was a super windy evening in the springtime. As I listened to all of the strange sounds in my home and began to wonder if our new house could withstand these strong winds. All the new noises and creaking sounds at my house were making made me nervous. I was hoping the sturdiness of our home wasn't like the house of sticks in the Three Little Pigs. I chose our home because of the peacefulness and serenity of the country. My backyard faces several cornfields and pastures of the surrounding farms. Very beautiful but also very open and no trees to block the winds.

My girls LOVED their trampoline. Every day the girls and I jumped together or them with their friends. It was the kind of trampoline with the safety netting around it.

This particular one had a really tightly woven mesh netting with a lot of tension to catch you if you fell onto the surrounding enclosure.

The winds were becoming even stronger the next morning. I was alarmed when I heard Morgan who was getting ready for school in a panicked scream, "Moooooomm, help!" I went running upstairs to see what was wrong. She said the trampoline is blowing away! I couldn't believe what I was seeing, this thing was so incredibly heavy yet it was rolling like a light little tumbleweed into the corn field behind our home. The winds literally picked up the trampoline because of tight weave of the netting which made it like a kite-like and lifted it off of the ground.

At one point I saw it go airborne and the tip of one leg was caught on the neighbors fence. It was teetering towards our neighbor's house and looked like it was being held in place in one little spot. It didn't look like it would take much to break free and fly into the house. I shouted my prayer, *Jesus help us right now, protect my neighbor please put the trampoline down and keep everyone safe.* I watched the trampoline as if by command settle to the ground and find a resting place right after I screamed my prayer. It was almost as if Jesus said instantly it's ok Donna, I am here.

When the winds died down we examined the trampoline to see if we could bend it back in shape. There was no coming back from the damage, it was bent beyond repair and looked like a twisted pretzel. I had to pay a service to saw it apart and remove it for me. My girls were heartbroken and wanted another one. Well that was an expensive trampoline and it would be a while for me to save for a new one.

I decided one day to put out a request, Universe can you please send us a used trampoline that comes to my attention for under $100 that would be delivered to my house free of charge. I kind of meant it as a joke, because that's asking pretty much. But I thought I would test my manifesting capabilities, why not put it out there and at least ask? I did not give it a second thought and didn't look for it to happen, but I didn't doubt it either.

It was maybe four weeks later there was a yard sale happening in my neighborhood. I had two different neighbors go out of their way to walk to my home ring my doorbell and say, hey did you know there is a trampoline for sale in the next neighborhood? (Knowing my girls lost theirs in the storm.) I asked where and decided to walk up the road to see if I could find it.

I saw it was actually someone we knew, my daughter Morgan's friends dad was selling their kids trampoline. It was a little older and a tad beat up, but it also had an enclosure. I asked how much he was asking he said $100. I asked if he would take $75? He said without hesitation sure! So I said to him, ok now I just have to figure out how to get it to my house, which wasn't far maybe less than 200 yards. He said I can bring it to you! He had a four wheeler and could hook the trampoline up to that, he said let me finish cleaning up here and I will bring it right down.

So I walked home and got out my checkbook and wrote out a check for $75. Within minutes I had a trampoline delivered to my backyard. Easy peazy! I realized later that day, hey wait a minute…. I had completely forgotten……I asked for this!

It had been brought to my attention just like I asked and I paid under $100, and it was delivered right into my backyard for free. Holy Moly! Check, check and check! All the boxes were ticked.

The thing that I observed with this manifestation was how I didn't sweat it. I didn't give it a second thought, I didn't say ohhh I wonder how the trampoline would show up? I really honestly forgot I asked for it and was completely unattached emotionally. I saw how easily without struggle it showed up for me literally delivered to my home as I requested. In contrast the situations or outcomes I was really attached to, like finding love, money seemed to stay at bay probably because I carried fear about those topics. Keeping it out of my reach for a bit.

Kind of like my desperately wanting a baby and coming at it from a place of not having it or lack. When I forgot to make God a part of the equation and relax knowing He is large and in charge, or when I tended to be emotionally attached and trying to control the outcome ~ my desires were delayed.

> *Ask…….have faith……..let it go…….allow it come the way*
> *it's supposed to come…….stay present and aligned…….*
> *and take guided or inspired action when prompted.*

CHAPTER 11

The Road To Better

I would like to share with you in this chapter some stories of how we can ask for help and recognize the answers of the divine. And in the light of day when there are times that you really don't like what is happening in your circumstances, sometimes it's best served to just make peace with where you are. Not forever, but resolve to just to BE for a bit until inspiration clearly strikes – or when you can see there is something for you to learn out of your situation. Do the best you can with where you are in the moment.

Have you ever experienced times where you felt completely exhausted from your efforts and you find yourself in the same exact place despite your best efforts? Or feeling like you are chasing an answer or solution spinning your wheels but you are left feeling scattered and lost? When you find yourself spinning, 'Stand ye still." Invite and allow the wisdom of life to find you.

Sometimes it would benefit you to take a look at what could be your role in the experiences you are facing that you don't love. To have and a willingness to be honest with yourself and others, to take a step back to look at the whole picture. And while you are at it, try working on your perceptions to a more optimistic filter or assess what you have been allowing into your life. Open your mind to new ways, new ideas or new solutions. And let's not forget the all important factor of making yourself a loving priority. Above all seek joy and appreciate the gifts in your journey as well. Life is not to just to be tolerated. And taking the time to focus on the energy of joy brings more of things you will love.

And help arrived ~

I promised you in the intro of this book I would share the story how Sherry woke up from the blame of her being the cause of Keith's abusive actions towards her. There are times we all could use a lifeline of support as Sherry did when we don't know where to turn and are searching for answers.

All of us at some point of our lives will experience hardship in different ways. Let's face it, it's not all rainbows and unicorns. Sometimes we even just need a little comfort knowing we are not alone. Asking the Universe for help during those difficult times can even be us asking for clarity and truth, not just our desires or outcomes. Helping us to determine the next right step or which way is best is ours for the asking!

Sometimes it maybe a small thing, and believe me you are not bothering Spirit with the little stuff. There is nothing too little. But there are moments where you may need help for something that is of a serious nature such as in Sherry's situation. In Sherry's mind the uncertainty laid in her decision that could alter her children's lives forever. As this was the only family her children have ever known. Sherry felt a need to be crystal clear around a few questions before taking any action to leave.

I have many people who come to me with circumstances where they are searching for answers. I simply say, "have you asked the Universe for clarity to help bring you peace and understanding?" To say, "please show me the right direction and the best answer and outcome for everyone in this situation." The response is usually the same, looking me deeply in the eye while they reflect...followed by a "no I haven't."

Invite the Universe in. You don't need to shoulder life's burdens, decisions, or solutions alone.

Often in abusive relationships the abuser blames the victim of the abuse for their actions. "If you would have said it this way" or "if you didn't do that, I wouldn't have reacted like that." "It's your fault how I treat you because of who you are and the things you do."

Worrying about your every action, every word you speak is exhausting. Living in fear of another person's reaction to your every move is a really terrible way to live and keeping you so incredibly small. You lose touch with who you truly are and lose the ability to know how you feel around simple topics.

Focusing on another person in every aspect of your existence is keeping you from your life purpose, from your own spirit and your divine right to a life of fulfillment. You lose your sense of self and the effect on your body and soul is weakening.

Sherry used to try to anticipate what her partner would want her to do or how to say something to keep him calm. She even struggled making choices at the grocery store. If she brought home one thing Keith decided they didn't need she would be belittled for days. No matter what she did her partner viewed it as was wrong.

Sherry kept asking for help in her prayers but she didn't seem to be getting rescued. She had this fantasy God would make it easy for her, that someone would see what was happening and get Keith out of the picture and it would be an instant fix. God would reach down pick up her partner and father to her children and replace him with a new and improved partner to love them in the ways she had dreamt a family should be. After not receiving any help or signs Sherry felt a bit abandoned.

When Sherry finally sat in stillness around this and quieting into her truth. She understood God is always with me, I have not been deserted. So why am I hearing nothing? What do you want from me God? What do I need to know?

Sherry felt a truth overcome her in her quiet reflection. She felt that God wanted her to see how strong she was, to rely on God and she wouldn't do this alone. Sherry knew she was going to have to muster up all of her inner strength to tell her biggest influence who was her family. No one ever saw her experience of what happened behind closed doors. She had to do this for her children, and herself regardless of others opinions. After her period of deep stillness and reflection, she came to a place of acceptance for where she was in the moment.

Sherry grew to understand she had to reframe what she was asking God. Her plea of "Heaven Help Me" didn't seem to bring results. She wanted to be clear of one thing before she would take any steps in good conscience. She asked God, is it me? Am I so messed up that I am acting in ways that I am not seeing? Is there any truth to I am causing him to do this to me? He said I abused him! Are you kidding? That really set her head spinning. She didn't see how. But she was willing to take a look at was it her.

Welcome to the neighborhood ~

Two thing happened that Sherry stated that she knew was Divine orchestration in answering her questions, "is it me?" First she got a new neighbor next door. Julie was a very intelligent psychologist from the south. Sherry had Julie over for tea one day just to welcome her to the neighborhood. That was their only interaction until one day Julie was at her fence and called her over.

Sherry was just returning from work and took her children outside to play. Her new neighbor motioned for her to come over. Sherry walked over to Julie who greeted her with a big friendly, "hello" followed by a very direct statement. "Your fiancé drives me nuts." Sherry felt herself uncontrollably smile. She thought to herself, I like her! Sherry then asked curiously, do you mind sharing why?

Julie proceeded to tell Sherry how controlling Keith was that day. While Sherry was at work the kids were playing outside while Keith worked on the lawn. He told them how to play, hovering over them, controlling their every move. Sherry looked at Julie and said, "OH you have no idea." Keith hadn't noticed he was being observed outside all day.

Sherry really opened up to Julie and began to confide to her some of her experiences. Julie said without hesitation, "that is abuse."

Julie then happened to look up and noticed Keith was standing in the window upstairs just watching them. Sherry said, "oh no, I am going to get it when I go inside." "He can tell I am talking about him." She felt sick and knew it would not be pleasant when she went into the house.

Since that day, Julie was an amazing support for Sherry. She went undetected like a fly on the wall she would stop some goings on in their path when they were happening. Julie didn't mind her own business thank God, as I know many people may turn the other way not wanting to get involved. Julie was such a huge help in Sherry gathering the strength to know this was not acceptable treatment she was experiencing. Finally Sherry didn't feel so alone.

One day after Sherry broke the news to Keith she wanted to end things, they began negotiations in the process of making plans to sell the house. Julie showed up knocking loudly at the back sliding door. Which was odd and impeccable timing. Sherry had been trapped and cornered for several minutes in the kitchen by Keith. Of course he bolted when the bold knock came at the door. Sherry looked at Julie knowing there was no accident in her timing.

Sherry opened the door and there her friend was, not a word just a smile and twinkle in her eye, only saying in that moment "hello dear." Sherry asked, "how did you know?" Julie replied, "your daughter came knocking on our door saying my mommy needs your help." "Daddy has my mommy trapped and he won't leave her alone." "Please come help my mommy."

So here was God sending someone to rescue her, remember her prayer? Sherry had already begun rescuing herself. Julie did rescue her in a sense by helping her see the truth without question. And she was no longer alone, and Sherry was provided the help of a strong intelligent woman who happened to move next door.

But Sherry got amazing reassurance in multiple signs when she reframed what she was asking. She got real with the truth of she was the one who needed to take the steps. No prince charming would show up to rescue her.

So maybe if you are not getting answers around any topic, think about *how* you are asking, and *what questions do you really need answered?*

An important question to Sherry was she needed to know before she made this life altering decision which would inevitably and irrevocably break up her family was, "is it me?" "What if I am a horrible person and not seeing it?" Sherry also asked God to make it easy to recognize the answer because she was not fantastic at identifying signs.

Believe me, you will know when it's your sign. At first you may question, I wonder if this is a message? When I began looking at signs I needed 3 times like Sherry did. I don't need 3 times these days. I can feel it with in me. You can do this as well simply put *asking and observing* into practice, being present and paying attention to what shows up throughout your day. You will build confidence and begin to trust and more easily identify answers.

3x a charm ~

Later that week Sherry needed to pick up her contacts at Walmart, so she dropped in on her way home from work. The line was super long, but she was on her last pair of contacts and really needed to get them that day. She got behind this super cute and friendly guy. They passed the next thirty minutes together having engaging conversations about what he did for a living.

He was a counselor to young inner city boys, keeping them out of trouble with after school activities. It was nice to see that there are kind, good men being of service. He was an admirable person doing good things to help kids in unfortunate circumstances. This guy told her about a basketball league he was involved in for the young boys. The idea was for the kids to come to the boys club after school not only because it was something fun, but it was also keeping the young boys off of the streets. Keeping them away from drugs and on a better path with positive role models. Sherry was truly having a nice time during this long wait.

It was his turn next. This guy paid and instead of leaving he approached Sherry and asked her out on a date. She laughed and said oh thank you, how flattering but I am engaged. He said oh I'm sorry, but you don't have on a ring. She explained she was having her rings repaired that week. He apologized, and said....

YOU ARE A REALLY NICE PERSON AND A GREAT GIRL, I REALLY HOPE YOUR FIANCE APPRECIATES YOU. DOES HE APPRECIATE YOU?

She of course said, yes he does. Sherry got out to her car and she thought about how she wasn't being honest with herself or with that man. Keith does not appreciate her or value her. She cried right there in the Walmart parking lot. She wondered if that was her sign? So she said to God, you know you have to hit me over the head with a brick (please don't, lol) but she wasn't sure if that was her sign. "God, can you please send me another sign to let me know if the problem is me?" "Thank you!"

A couple of days later Sherry took her oldest daughter to this wonderful place she found to take an art class in town. The owners mother often would come down from the neighboring county which was about an hour away. The mother enjoyed to just socialize with her daughter and their clientele. Sherry and the mother had one of their many enjoyable conversations, laughing and connecting. The mom looked at Sherry and said in a very sincere way....

YOU ARE THE NICEST GIRL, YOU ARE SUCH A GOOD PERSON, I REALLY HOPE YOU FIANCE APPRECIATES YOU! DOES HE APPRECIATE YOU?

Ok, now this time Sherry felt stopped in her tracks, almost as if hearing the twilight zone music on cue. Pretty much the same words two times in one week. So many of you would way that's enough. There's your message! She began to question God, "was that a pretty big coincidence or was this a message?"

Sherry said, "Ok God, one last time please." "If the problem is not me can you please just give me one more sign." "I am sorry, but I need to make sure please don't get frustrated with me." Side note here, I had read that when you hear a message 2 or 3 times you need to pay attention - there is definitely a message trying to be relayed to you. Sherry wasn't at 3 yet. A side note here is we tend to humanize God and the angels. They don't get sick of us I promise.

That weekend Sherry's daughter had a basketball game at her Elementary School. It was a big challenge to have her little toddler sit still courtside on those hard, cold folding chairs. Her son wanted to run onto the court and play basketball with the big kids. Sherry decided go into the hallway where her son could run freely and she could also watch her older daughter's game at the same time.

Sherry struck up a conversation with nicest grandparents of the opposing team while letting her son have a bit of freedom to run the halls. She can't even recall what they talked about but they were having a great time chatting. After about 30 minutes, the couple said to Sherry ... yes, yes it happened again...

> ***YOU ARE SO DOWN TO EARTH, YOU ARE SUCH A NICE PERSON WE SURE HOPE YOUR FIANCÉ APPRECIATES WHAT HE HAS IN YOU.***

There she had it, three times in one week. Almost word for word the same statement. She had her answer. Sherry thanked the God for His patience.

Riding home in the car she had a feeling of such celebration that she really got her signs around the questions she had prayed about. But also in this moment she was experiencing a duality of feelings. One reality was heaven actually was helping her which made her feel totally elated and supported! The other reality was understanding the path that lays ahead may be unpleasant while reaching for a better life.

Sherry walked every day with God on this path knowing she had her answer. Today Sherry and her children live a fabulously joyful life. Where she and her children have freedom to be themselves and to love openly, and live peacefully.

Eric and Italy too!!

So fast forward to dating years after my own divorce, when a guy I just started seeing took me to a Smokey Robinson concert at the casinos in Atlantic City. He asked what other concerts I would like to see. There was some concert he was interested in seeing in Italy, he asked if I would go to Italy with him? I said YES how fun! We saw each other only about 6 weeks. I realized we weren't very unenthusiastic about each other in truth. I knew he wasn't my person so I thought what am I really doing? I wasn't really enjoying myself.

At this stage of the game I said you know what God, I think I am done with men. I realized I needed to heal some things within me, as an Energy Teacher I understood what was showing up in my experiences was simply a reflection of my inner world. I need to be by myself maybe for bit, or maybe for a lifetime. Who knows? I just couldn't seem to get the relationship thing right and really didn't trust the decisions I was making. I really wasn't feeling it for anyone who crossed my path dating wise.

I realized when I sat with what was being reflected back to me energetically that I wasn't making myself a priority. Therefore - no one else did either! It was clear to me I needed to get my energy to gorgeously expansive levels of self love if I wanted to experience being loved.

One day I said with all seriousness, it's You and me God, I guess I had my chance at marriage. I am not good at finding the right person, so maybe you have other things you want for my life. You are in large and in charge. I'm done trying to be in control of the navigation. I will take it day by day, You, my kids, loving myself better, my wine (lol) and my girlfriends. That's it. Unless you have someone for me, but it has to come from you. I'm out. I ask if by chance, if you find someone for me that somehow I clearly know YOU sent them. I ask you put him directly in my path because I am NOT looking and I am completely done with dating sites. Otherwise, I will just "be" and accept I am to be by myself.

I also decided I don't need a man to take me to Italy. I followed up my last statements with, "Universe please take me on an all expense paid trip to Italy, thank you!" Again laughing kind of like I did with the trampoline not giving it a second thought. In regards to relationships, I have heard people say to find your person you have to not try. I have witnessed this with clients. The ones who were really happy in their marriages and who I knew themselves had struggled to find a good relationship until they met their husbands.

Beyond the concept of not trying, I came to the conclusion the common denominator was they started just having fun, or making *themselves* their focus. Self-love and really connecting to self-fulfillment and their own path. My entire career in the beauty business I have been an observer of energy and how we create our lives and the unfolding.

One client had her heart broken when her guy didn't want to be committed to her and broke up with her. She was very sad, but picked herself up and just focused on fun with her friends. He saw her out one night after they were broken up for a several months and he noticed something different about her. Something about her had changed. She didn't need him, she didn't pay any attention to him. She was in the moment, loving life and her girlfriends, dancing and laughing, so carefree. He found this change very attractive. He couldn't stay away, they were engaged very quickly and now have 3 kids.

Another client of mine who had the looks of a supermodel whose insides were just as beautiful. She told me of her woes with same thing, commitment phobe partners who left her disappointed. Always the observer of energy and perspective, I asked what she felt changed within her before she met her at this point fiance. She said she started focusing on herself. Renovating and decorating her home, really enjoying making her home so beautiful. She was truly happy in enjoying her own company and doing things that were fulfilling to her.

Both girls made themselves the focus. Not in a narcissistic way, but in a self-care and I matter way. So what showed up was a reflection that they were worthy of time and focus. They were in a state that was a loving and happy self-fulfilled vibration. What they attracted in a relationship was a loving mate, because they were loving themselves! Remember LIFE IS A MIRROR!

I had tried to practice this in the past, but I didn't really mean it. Kind of pretending, Ok Universe....here's me over here, valuing myself, I let gooooo. See me letting go? LOL, not! I always was attached in some way to some guy making THEM the source of my happiness. But THIS time I meant it to my core. I felt with every fiber of my being, it was time. I had to choose to live from an authentic space honoring and loving myself in every thought, every action and interaction.

At this point of my life, I again had allowed a guy to not value me not in the same way of other relationships, but I accepted less than I deserved for 5 years. I made the mistake of making his happiness my goal. I wasn't my focus, again.

By comparison of other relationships, the other significant relationship in my life was a much better level. He was a very quiet reserved man. I was caught up in the deep love I felt. He wined and dined me, took me to exciting places, and made all the plans which I felt very treasured in that sense. But he played some games with me because of his fears which wreaked havoc on me emotionally. I did a lot of hoop jumping to make him happy. But to me at the time, it was way better than my last long term relationship.

I got serious about doing some real reflecting. I became clear how I treated myself, where everyone came before me. Me last always in my own thoughts and actions. I always worried was everyone else happy but not about my own needs. No accident that this would be what showed up in my world. Whether I chose him or someone else, the energy of where I was in my core belief about self would be reflected back to me. It was what I attracted in my experience.

I decided no exceptions....new focus today... self-love, self-love, self-love! Which is really truly about a new level of deep self-care, being 100% authentic to myself with intense dedication. 24/7.

I also accepted it was going to hurt for a bit while I healed from losing my 5 year boyfriend. I actually accepted this had peace around it. I was going to be completely committed to myself and diving head first with extreme self care. I firmly told myself:

I am now truly taking responsibility for what is showing up in my life from here on out I am not a victim, but rather the creator of the story and take responsibility for the energy I hold. If I don't like what's showing up I better work on my core beliefs and my energy with great love and passion for myself.

I spent many a day and night by myself in this new town mending my heartbreak. But simultaneously sending love to myself for where I was. I was fully present in each moment *allowing the pain and not distract myself from feeling it fully. As when you avoid the energy of what you are feeling, it stays in our minds, body and energy.... we are not clearing or releasing it.*

We as humans often look for a better feeling so we don't feel uncomfortable. Which is good and appropriate at times as we have to be present at work or when we are busy with family. But continuing to suppress uncomfortable feelings that need to come up to be healed and released can keep us stuck in that same energy we are trying to avoid and not feel.

Continuing to avoid feeling the feelings that what we don't love is how we keep attracting similar situations. We will continue until we finally give the energy and the emotions presenting themselves the attention it needs to clear it and change our outer experiences.

As my mentor Louise would say in our teacher trainings, that's fine if you choose to ignore what's showing up for you....but do you want to go another lap around the track? It will get louder and louder in your experiences until you just can't go down that path again. Until we choose ourselves to deal with the very thing we are avoiding feeling. Clear it and instead choose better ways of being, choose you.

My focus was working very hard at my new job and studied often for my new product lines to give perfect presentations. I totally enjoyed my time with my kids, being in the moment with them and having fun in every moment together. The pain managed to surface a bit more when no one was around. I allowed myself to feel this sadness, no self judgement, just feeling it. And that was ok, the best medicine for healing and self-love is to feel what you need to fully. To deal with courage the uncomfortableness of the energy coming up to be released. The other side of this is pain is relief and freedom!

So I thought I was done ~

When I'd see a cute guy who was giving me attention, and I'd say nope Donna you know the drill. God it's just me and you, I told myself to keep walking. This became a common and dedicated practice. Until one day I went to go to the gym at my complex where I lived. I had an access card that went haywire that week. It wouldn't let me in at 6:30 a.m. I tried many times with no luck, so there I stood locked outside the empty little gym gazing at all of the equipment inside. I decided to power walk before I start my day to at least in a little exercise. So I popped my earbuds in and set to walking where I lived.

I looped a few times around the complex and on the last loop I saw a man loading up his SUV. He turned his head and I could tell he saw me walking in his direction. I could feel it, oh CRAP....he's going to talk to me. Knowing better than to pay attention to boys these days I did an eye roll, and said Oh Godddd! Keep in mind I feel energy of people's authenticity, integrity very easily. I have no tolerance for BS at this point. None.

This man turned around and said, "Good Morning how are you?" "Are you new here?" We did some introductions. Immediately this man's energy was supremely different than most people I have ever met. Very pure, positive and booming dynamic energy. Within seconds I put down my wall of I don't want to talk to you. He was TOTALLY my kind of person!

We continued to chat for a few minutes and I walked away feeling really happy and open, like someone I had shared a lifelong friendship. I felt a pull towards this person I only spoke to for maybe less than 10 minutes. I thought boy I really need a friend. Maybe I should ask him to go out for a drink sometime, he reminds me of my college buddies. Then my next thought was keep walking Donna, you know the drill. You are done. He will think you want him and you don't want to give him the wrong idea, no boys remember? Nevermind I thought.

That weekend I saw Eric about 8 feet in front of my living room window shouting up to his friend who lived above me. My instinct was to burst open the door like hey how are you? But again, I said to myself nope, he will think you want him so don't you open that door Criqui.

Jadin woke up and walked out to the living room seeing Eric outside our window. She said who is that? I said his name is Eric, he is really nice I met him in the parking lot on a walk this week. She said he sure has a lot of muscles. I laughed, he did. He was a bodybuilder and competed at one point, he was quite huge.

The next weekend Jadin was with her dad, and Morgan was working in Reading, Pennsylvania. I had the whole weekend to myself. My friend Deb invited me to her house but it was over an hour drive. I had some work to do for a project and I wanted to nail my presentation on Monday.

I was working inside my tiny apartment until about 1 p.m. when I just started sobbing. God I am so lonely and so sad. Please send me a friend today, I really could use a friend and I miss my girls. Still very heartbroken about leaving my dream home with the man I had loved so deeply and thought I would marry.

Suddenly I felt an inner prompting very clearly just go to the pool, get some sunshine and take a break. I thought ok, I can spare a half an hour get a little fresh air and sunshine. That will do me some good! Looking back

I feel like the idea came from out of nowhere and it came very inspired and urgently, go, go, go, go. So I wiped my tears, put on my bikini and off I went.

I got to the pool and sat next to two ladies. We eventually started chatting and I had a really nice conversation with a mom and her daughter for a while. I began to feel a little lighter. Next thing I knew I saw what looked like Eric coming around the fence, I said to myself, oh I think this is Eric with his kids! He rounded the corner and it was him. I found myself fixing my bathing suit and my primping my hair when he wasn't looking. I observed my actions questioning myself, what are you doing Donna?? I think you like him!!

I sat with myself around that, because you know my rule. I'm done. But I started to recognize I felt excited to see to him. Eric and I had the best time talking that day at the pool, really heartfelt, funny, deep conversations all over the board of topics. My plans were only going to the pool for 30 minutes, but I ended up staying for 3 hours. I just didn't want to leave the awesome time I was having and felt at home for the first time moving to New Jersey. And I was just enamored with Eric's little girl who was too adorable and I spent quite some time chatting with her too.

I noticed her bathing suit and asked if it was from the store Justice. She said how did you know? I told her I have a daughter who shopped there as well. She seemed to take a shine to me too. His son was a little wild man who was too cute as well, being louder than his sister, splashing and jumping with his dad as he spoke to me. Eric mentioned that a bunch of people go out to a place on the water in Delaware called Firebirds and asked if I wanted to go sometime. I said I would like to. I thought I really would like to make more friends around here. Even though I was moving back to Reading, PA in about 6 weeks.

During our conversations I mentioned my daughter Morgan. Eric said, oh you have a Morgan? That's Morgan pointing to his little girl. He next asked me, what's your other daughters name. I said Jadin. He just paused, looked me dead in the eye pointed to his son and said, that's Aden! We both looked at each other with no words for what seemed like a long time.

So Morgan and Aden, Morgan and Jadin. Hmmm.... Universe? What are you trying to telling me here? That definitely caught my attention, and I found out much later it really caught Eric's as well. We both knew something special was happening in us being together that day.

The following week I was returning from my Dr. appointment about halfway up my sidewalk when Eric pulled up behind me and parked in front of my apartment. He stopped to say hello and asked if I wanted to go to Firebirds in Delaware that he had told me about. I said sure that would be fun. I handed him my business card and wrote my number on back. So I thought there would be a bunch of us that were going out, because that's what he originally said. I started getting texts from Eric asking do you like comedy clubs? What kind of food do you like, do you like seafood? I began to think, boy this sounds like a date kind of questions.

I got to work at the salon that night and said to my friend Kate, so I'm not sure, I think I have a date. She said you *think*? How do you not know? I told Kate how it went down. I showed her his pic on FB. I liked him a lot as a person, I began to ponder this being an actual date with this man. I finally asked him if anyone else was going with us. He replied NO! I laughed. I questioned my no guy rule, but really felt I should go. Funny thing is if it was clear it was a date when Eric asked, I most likely would have said no. But the way it went down I just laughed.....I could see the Universe's hand at play.

Long story short, there were so many signs as we went out over the next few weeks. I kept Eric at arm's length while dating for the first 6 months being cautious. But I totally lived in the moment and kept checking in with my heart to see what God was telling me about this relationship when I got scared. Eric over 4 years later still brings me so much joy, we laugh a lot, we still have the deepest conversations and he shows me how much he cares often. More than I had ever had within a relationship.

Remember when I asked God, if you have someone please put him in my path. He literally was in my walking path. Remember when I asked for a way to know undeniably God has his hand in it. There were so many signs. Our kids names were just what caught our attention, but many more signs came that knocked my socks off.

Funny thing was before I gave up on men, I had written down all of my qualities I wanted in a mate. At one of my angel classes the teacher told us how very quickly she called in her husband by making a detailed list and carried it in her purse. My best friend Brenda who attended the same angel class decided to create her own list of what she wanted immediately after that class. She gave the list to God in prayer and very quickly met her husband. Only to find out while dating her husband that he himself made his own list to call in his person. The jaw dropping synchronicity is they both made their lists *the exact same day*. September 25. And both of them totally fulfilled each other's list completely. They are happily married for 4 years.

Several weeks before I had tucked my list in my purse as the angel teacher advised. I completely had forgotten that I even made it. It was after I had made my list when I said to God I am done with men and leave my path up to You. I found my list about a month after Eric and I started dating when I was organizing my purse. I checked it out to see what I wrote, I totally couldn't remember what the details were.

Do you believe Eric hit every single one of the qualities and more of what I desired in a relationship. Right down to the beautiful smile, and straight teeth and athletic manly build, funny, loves family, would love my girls in a fatherly way, a strong love of God, he doesn't have to believe what I believe but accepts who I am in my ways to God. Someone who wants a monogamous and committed relationship, makes time for me and much more.

Time to get a passport ~

So now what about Italy? Remember the guy who said he would take me Italy but then I realized he just wasn't my person. I thought I am not making him the source of me going to Italy! Within 6 months of me asking Universe please send me on a trip to Italy, I was told by work I was being sent to Italy in a few months!

The Hair color company I had just begun to educate for is based out of Italy. They never had educators from the USA there for training. It just so happened that this year they just decided to host an International Educator Training at corporate headquarters. And I was invited to go! It was the most exquisite trip of my life. The most beautiful venues and restaurants, I fell more in love with the company by going to our corporate headquarters. Style, passion and class with a beautiful heart! They treated us like royalty with so much appreciation and respect. The decadence, fun, laughter and friendships I made from all around the world from that trip was so fantastic.

I was honored to be included with this group of accomplished hairdressers and heads of companies from around the world. My heart was bursting! So let me tell you to date, I will be going this year for the fourth time to Italy. I am humbled and grateful this year that this year I was also given the gift of being asked to represent the United States on stage for the cutting and color segment at our huge International Hair Show as a part of the Global Team. The Wish that keeps on giving!

Trust the process is one of my favorite statements, because at times circumstances may not look great or feel great in the moment. But the story is not done my friends. It doesn't end with your undesirable circumstances of this moment. You are in process and things are in motion, even when it appears things are standing still.

Why not try to let go of the way you think things should look in your mind right now, knowing there are things happening behind the scenes that you may not see coming just yet. Remember the Universal Wisdom that keeps all the planets running perfectly is in charge of the grand picture unfolding for you as well. You never know what awaits.

My lessons and takeaway

So I learned something here. Getting what I had asked for came in its proper timing when I stopped pushing and forcing. I finally came to a place where I trusted that better may lay outside how I wanted things to be. I felt lost in my life for a while. I was really was unhappy with my circumstances and in a great deal of pain and uncertainty. I totally accepted this is where I was in the moment.

Instead of having a tantrum or complaining, I just simply said ok. It's just the way things are right now. I didn't have to do a thing but take care of me and work on loving myself in new and beautiful ways. Every day I said ok God, I am going to give my best to each day and live in the moment and allow what it is you wish for me to do. I am giving my path to you, please take me where you want me to go. I don't even know what goals to set or what to ask You for right now! I am completely trusting and am in Your care.

I didn't miss my good by letting go completely and focusing on other areas of my life. To the contrary, it all came right to me! Italy, the trampoline, and Eric.

As challenging of times I have had, these little and not so little miracles remind me it's ok to ask, to set your intentions, but also trust in the bigger plan and the best outcome. The best may not be what you are thinking. It will unfold with grace when we step back and don't insist on a certain way.

If something doesn't happen say thank you, God may have something way more extraordinary than you EVER imagined. Know that something better is on the way or the timing is working itself out perfectly. But remember the road to better begins with us. Empower yourself with faith, allow yourself to breathe and put yourself in HIS care and also your own best care. Letting go of our control puts us on a miraculous path paved by the Universe in its eminent wisdom. Enjoy observing the unfolding.

Chapter 12

Surrender

What does it mean to surrender? Well to me it means when I let go 100% to the Divine Hand and Universal wisdom. To totally hand over the direction I will be taken. Trusting when I have surrendered that God will bring me to the highest and best outcome, even if I don't love where I am. Leaving all of the details and the unfolding completely to God's care without my backseat driving. Really most times we surrender because something seems too big for little ol' us or we have no idea how to even begin. Or maybe we have tried to do something ourselves and the outcome wasn't pleasing.

More often than not, we can't control situations and definitely not people and their actions. We can only control ourselves, our choices, our perspectives, how we choose to be in our own integrity and our own actions. We think we are figuring things out by obsessing over things from a mental plane. From a mental space we really are only limiting the outcome to only our own thinking, and that vicious loop of energy keeps circling with in our body and perpetuating feelings of disparity. My bets are with God and the Divine plan above mine every time.

Getting in the habit of trusting and letting go is VERY FREEING! We let go in the energy of rounding the same pattern of worrying with in our body which is a contractive energy. By surrendering, we go beyond ourselves and into the beautiful expansive unlimited, all-inclusive energy of God. Giving all the details to our Divine all-knowing Source, and allowing the unfolding and trying not to judge the happenings as they unfold. Absolutely do your part to the best of your abilities, but let God handle the rest.

This allows you to get on with life and enjoy the present. If you have handed something over, knowing whatever shows up from this point….. is higher wisdom. I know you can see where I have surrendered in a few of my stories, and I am sure there are times you can recall for yourself where this act is incredibly powerful.

I have always wanted to empower my girls. Encouraging them to be the best version of themselves and do their part in creation. To cultivate with in them a strength, creativity, value the importance of education, a strong work ethic and believing in themselves. I wanted to model that for them by example. There were times since our divorce my girls mentioned things were different in their friends homes who had two parents. I could tell they wished for more.

I made sure we celebrated our special love and I told them I felt we were so lucky in so many ways. I had to get creative financially when we couldn't do all the things their friends did with two working parents. I explained there is always someone with more, and always someone with less. I treasured our beautiful love in our tight little unit and our bonds are so strong. Our relationships with friends and family were abundant, we laughed open hearted fun belly laughs and shared quick witted humor.

Over the years their friends have said they to like to come to our home. Many of my daughter's friends have called me mom. We have lots of love and acceptance for who they were, which for kids it is so important as they are in the process in discovering more about self and how to be in the world.

An area I felt some pressure was to help my girls feel a sense of belonging when they entered the teen years. I was them wanting to get them certain things that everyone else had and do things that there friends were able to do easily. I heard from time to time why does this person have 3 ipods (my how times have changed, right?), they just got another ipad, the latest iphone and are going to Disney AGAIN? I told Morgan years ago when she wanted a $60 sweatshirt from Hollister the answer at times was "yes, but not today."

I wanted to empower my girls how to be hopeful and resourceful for themselves but also to build a relationship with the God. And to teach them to recognize when the Universe is responding to their prayers.

Sometimes being a single parent the how's seemed overwhelming and unreachable for me to provide their desires. They were good kids, and really deserved so much that I could not provide own my own. I decided to teach my girls a valuable lesson that hopefully they could carry with them as a lesson for their own tool belt. I decided to teach them a way of asking and surrendering in a fun way to ask for the fulfillment of their dreams to a much higher power than myself.

The vision board project success

My girls and I enjoyed doing art and crafts together since they were tiny little things. One New Year's Day I gathered poster board, scissors and glue and sat my girls down on our living room floor. I asked them what would they love to show up in their lives if they could have anything they wanted. What a fun time to playfully ponder and speak about their hopes and dreams with such shared excitement. After we discussed their desires with some flowery details we then went to the computer. We found and printed pictures that represented their desires off of google image searches. Cut, paste and stick!

This first step was to teach my girls how tap into the deepest desires of their heart and get clarity around that. Having fun describing the details tapping into their imaginations. Once we were done what seemed like a fun art project, we invited God and the angels in and we asked for us all to receive our desires surrendering them over to the Universe. I didn't have the knowledge of how I could provide all of the things they wanted or I wanted for them. But I sure knew the power of asking and surrendering.

I decided to teach my girls how to have an interactive relationship with God and how we can put things in motion by asking. From there it is not our job to figure out how our requests will happen, it's the Universe's job. Our job is to identify clearly what we would like to experience in our lives and hand it over. I made it fun, lighthearted, and age appropriate for my young girls. I had made vision boards in the past, but the ones we did this particular day were powerful. My girls were 15 and 9 years old.

From this particular project, Morgan and I had some pretty cool manifestations. Morgan wanted a horse and a mastiff. I had put on my board a free car for Morgan who would soon be 16 years old. Morgan said to me one day, hey Mom I received what I asked for from our vision board but in a different way than what I thought.

Morgan became close friends with a friend of mine who owns and operates an animal rescue, The Almost Home Sanctuary. I met Tara through my reiki teacher Carol. Both of my daughter's would come with me to her farm to visit. Morgan really connected with Tara's humor and mutual love of animals.

I would have to work a of couple evenings at the salon, so two evenings a week I wasn't home until 8 or 9 p.m. At this point Morgan chose to live with me full time. I didn't want Morgan to get lonely when I had to work my evenings. We were so lucky that Tara welcomed Morgan to come spend time with her at her home and animal rescue.

Tara has many mastiff's and also had a horse on her farm. Tara invited Morgan to not only spend much of her free time visiting and helping, but also spent the better part of many weekends on Tara's farm. Morgan got super close to a gigantic and sweet Mastiff named Gnocchi. Gnocchi would howl in a way that sounded likes cries of protesting when Morgan would leave to come back home. They were quite the pair and just loved each other so much. His head was 3 times the size of Morgan's and outweighed my daughter by about 60 pounds, but this enormous dog turned to gush when he saw my girl.

Not only did Morgan get to sleep over and cuddle Gnocchi in his room (yes he had his own bedroom), she also got to ride a horse named Bacon and loved to help care for him. Morgan's pointed out to me one day her desires for a mastiff and a horse were fulfilled plus it didn't cost me a dime. I love how this not only showed up for her but also how Morgan herself is the one recognized the Universe supported her in ways outside of our thinking. The power of having clarity, asking the Universe and then letting it go and allowing. We did not own the animals, but they were a part of Morgan's everyday life.

I'll take a Volvo with all the trim ~

So when Morgan turned 16 years old I let her get a tattoo to symbolize something meaningful to her. Morgan drew the tattoo herself, she is such an amazing artist. It was only $150 and this was something she really wanted for her special birthday, and something I could swing budget wise. My requirement was I need to approve of it, you have to give it careful thought and it should be something you would be proud of when you are 40 years old, represent who you are, and be hidden because you are under 18 years old.

We posted Morgan's new tattoo on Facebook, and she was ecstatic! The artist did the most wonderful job, she got the Tree of Life. The leaves on the tree seemed to come to life. Being an artist myself I appreciated the details of her tattoo. I studied the highlight, and shading within the artwork. It was very beautifully done.

So fast forward to my cousin Jimmy's 60th birthday celebration in Philadelphia that weekend - I was chatting with my brother Mike. He said what's up with Morgan getting a tattoo? He had seen it on his wife's Facebook page. I said, "Look I can't afford to get a car for Morgan or throw her a big party, so this was something she really wanted." "And I don't have a problem with it." Mike said about that, his son Christopher is getting a new car.... *how would you like to have his old car for Morgan?*

About 6 months prior I put on my vision board a free car for Morgan. Not only was it a free car, it was an older Volvo! Black with a tan leather interior. It was a bit loved and broken in, but it was gorgeous and a safe car and free. Thank you Mike, you have no idea what that meant to us. And wow, another vision board manifestation fell into our laps. This is a tool of creation friends. And really it is an act of asking and surrendering!

I just had a friend who is also a client reach out to me last night asking for guidance how to do a vision board. She knew I had had some great success with them in the past. The key is clarity, sitting around what is important to you. You begin to daydream, explore and go deep within yourself. Next you search for pictures that get you excited and represent your desired end result. It could be from a magazine, or pictures you find on google.

I myself have put things into categories. But that was my personal touch. Such as a spiritual category with where I want to improve, or a romance category what I would love to experience, Career Success section, Money Section, Family and my Kids section. I have filled in even with words I printed off of the computer, and searched. But it's simple, no hard fast rules in the how. Clarity, gather pics, paste, and go into your heart/spirit to pray sending out your intention and release it to God. Then go on with life, enjoy. Don't worry about it. Remember fear or doubt or worrying about it creates resistance. KNOW it's coming. I always like to say "I ask for this or something better." Because who knows, God could have something way beyond your best dreams!

Revisit what's on your board from time to time and tap into the feeling of having your dreams. And then remember to let go of the how's. And just simply allow the path unfold for you and remain unattached as well. You can simply say to yourself, I don't know how it's going to show up, I don't need to see the process. I am excited to see how it comes!

Acceptance and surrender

I heard something at a my Charles Virtue class that I already knew. But for some reason there is a time you are ready to hear the message. You hear the same thing you heard a 1000 times but this time something clicks. You finally get it. You take it into your consciousness on a new and deeper level. Charles asked at the class, what have you been saying (referring to the power of our words.)... and continued to ask us to take a look around you, what have you been experiencing?

I thought about it for under a minute, what have I been saying? I was always afraid I would not have enough to care for my girls and myself. I had been saying over and over to my friends, I'd rather be poor and happy than married to my ex-husband. Well guess what, I was poor and happy and not married to my ex-husband! LOL!

Clearly I needed to change my story and my words. But in all of my experiences with lessons around my role with God, I was given an opportunity for my faith to grow and received very impactful lessons. I saw how heaven does help us, and noticed everyday miracles. I also saw eventually *my role* in the grand scheme of things. And my next story I learned a lesson around the power of acceptance and surrendering what you are facing.

That will be $6,000 to fix your car!

I had a really cute used white Wolfsberg edition Volkswagen Passat. Loaded with a killer sound system, moonroof, and heated leather seats. I loved my cool little car. It was very stylish with sophistication which was something I truly enjoyed. I was able to find a car I loved that was affordable by going the used car route. I had a warranty until 50,000 miles and don't you know I had an expensive breakdown happen at around 51,000 miles.

I took my Passat to my dealership for the repair. The estimate was somewhere to the tune of $6,000. I was completely horrified. I owed enough on my loan balance that I couldn't trade in my car. That would be an insane car payment. I asked the dealership do you have a recall on anything with my car....are you sure I'm not covered for this? Right there in front of me they did some research and found there was no recall for my VIN. And then they reminded me my warranty was only good until 50,000 miles.

I swore most technical things had a self-destruct timer when you were out of warranty. Like there is someone in a remote location sitting behind a panel seeing a red flashing light signaling that you are out of warranty. They press a big red button and say.....ok breakdown NOW!

I left wondering what I could do. I remembering sweating the whole scenario, finally after praying for a few days and not really feeling like anything was changing nor was I seeing any signs or positive movement. I was getting pressure from the dealership to make a decision, I couldn't keep using the loaner they gave me for a few days. After many moments of silence and praying for guidance I came to a conclusion.

Ok God, I guess I need to accept where I am. And I have no choice, so I will get it fixed. We will just live off of peanut butter and jelly sandwiches for like a year, I guess we won't have Christmas. I will have to tell the girls this is just what we have to do for now. I *really accepted* this would be our life for now. I said to God wholeheartedly, you have always taken care of us. You always will. I had this short conversation with God in the little Jetta loaner I was given on my way into work that foggy fall morning.

I arrived at the salon about 10 minutes after I said, "Ok God you always take care of us, I am willing to survive off of peanut butter and jelly sandwiches and not having Christmas presents for my girls." I planned on making that dreaded call when I had time between clients that day. Leanne our receptionist at Bailiwick said to me as soon as she saw me, Donna the Volkswagen dealer just called. She then handed me the phone number and told me they said it's important, to give them a call back asap.

I dialed the phone with a pit in my stomach curious to see why the dealership reached out, I wasn't expecting a phone call. I thought they were just going to press me for a decision. Instead I heard, *"Donna, you are not going to believe this. I went look up your car this morning on the computer, and Volkswagen just extended the warranty on your model of car to 100,000 miles just now."* He didn't know how it happened because he was the one who researched my warranty right in front of me just the other day. But today the warranty was unexpectedly changed by Volkswagen to 100,000 miles. He said let's get this started right away before anything changes, it's paid in full. Zero dollars out of your pocket.

I had a stunned look on my face as I hung up the phone and was silent. I simply stood there reviewing what just had unfolded in my world. My friend Leanne asked what happened, as she knew my dilemma and saw the look on my face. I told her I no longer have to pay $6,000. Moments after I said God you always take care of me. I'll do my part and accept where I am. Please walk with me.....and woah. Within 10 minutes I received a miracle that even the dealership didn't know what happened. I mean I knew when I bought the car the warranty was good until 50,000. It wasn't an oversight and now suddenly I am covered to 100,000 miles.

Not resisting the reality and acceptance for where I was to me was a big lesson. Stating God knows what He is doing, call Him in, let Him work what he needs to work out and know He is always with you. Surrender (the energy of letting go or non-resistance) and let God take care of the rest. You do your part by inviting God in, then let God show you how awesome His wisdom and grace is!

I Give Her to YOU!!!

I met a man couple of years into being single was who I thought would be my forever person. He was from NJ and I met him on Fitness Singles. He and I dated on and off for 5 years. Many lessons I learned from my time with him. My goal was to have a complete family with a really solid father figure for my girls. He bought a beautiful lake home for us in NJ, the girls for the summer would be splitting their time between PA and the new home and hour and a half apart.

Morgan was 18 years old and sharing time at her boyfriend's family home and ours while she was trying to decide if she would attend college in NJ or PA. She took a year off after high school while she was deciding and worked part time. I really missed when my girls were an hour and a half away when they were not with me. I was used to sharing my time in a divorce situation with a less than 5 minute distance from their dad when they would spend time with him. Morgan however was with me 24/7 since deciding at 14 years old to live with me full time. Jadin still shared half of her time with her father.

One night shortly after the move to the new home I woke up with an awful feeling, like it was being laid upon my whole being. I understand what a "knowing" feels like. I felt impending doom for Morgan that woke me out of a sound sleep. The feeling was so intensely strong and a thought omg.... Morgan is going to die and be taken from me!

At first I blamed it on me not being used to the distance between us, I tried to brush it off as me overreacting but realized it was being shown to me in my energy and in my body. This horrid feeling of she was going to die was not subsiding, I was going to lose her. Such danger she was in, I completely and fully felt it. The feeling was like a cloud of prophecy that terrified me to my core.

I began to pray around 3 a.m. fervently.... help Morgan protect her, God, Jesus, Archangel Michael, Mary, take care of her PLEASE!! The feeling wasn't letting up. So finally I remember Charles Fairchild my client telling me lay it at the foot of the cross, give it to Him and don't take it back. Surrendering means you need to leave it there. I mentioned this story earlier how Charles at his one appointment upon paying for his bill handed me the construction nail he carried in his pocket to remind him to leave it at the foot of the cross. Leave it there at Jesus' feet.

I couldn't get this feeling out of me, I kept praying she's yours God take her completely. I am not going to even be so illusioned I can do anything, I don't want control and won't take any control. I give her up to you totally. I felt to imagine physically reaching into my body and pull all of my concerns out of me and gave Morgan completely to my vision of God energetically.

I kept reaching until I finally felt I let go of me having any worries over this. I pictured Morgan with God, Him holding my special girl so safely. Morgan is God's I told myself, that's all I can do. I had completely surrendered.

About 30 hours later on Friday morning, I noticed I was receiving a call on my cell phone shortly after arriving to work. I was about 2 weeks into starting over after 25 years of hairdressing in Berks County, now working as a stylist at Verde Salon in NJ. I looked closer at my cell phone ringing on this beautiful summer morning in July, it was Morgan. I said to a coworker, this is not normal for my daughter to reach out this early, I should take this. Surprised, but not really surprised. Feeling like OMG here it is, this is about my premonition....I took a deep breath as I walked outside. The first thing Morgan said was hi, I could hear from the "hi" she was scared and sounded extremely weak.

I immediately sat down on a bench knowing I had to brace myself. After her weak hello Morgan said to me, "just so you know I am ok." Morgan told me she was in a very bad accident the night before and her car was completely totaled. She was banged up a bit but alright, nothing broken.

I told Morgan immediately after hearing her news that I was coming to be with her. Morgan said I didn't need to come, but I knew us. I knew she needed me, and I needed to hold her. I was nervous to tell my new job I needed to leave the state to go get my girl, but I immediately left for PA.

The ride home was pretty shaky for me, processing the happenings and the feeling I had the other night that Morgan was going to die. Within 18 hours of me being woken with a premonition out of a dead sleep, her car was totaled but she was alive. God saved my girl, I know it to the depth of my being.

Morgan and I chatted on my ride to her to comfort each other. She told me the story of what happened, how she felt it was her time as it was happening and said to herself....ok, I am going to die. She said was actually at peace about it. I forgot to mention, yes I gave Morgan to God, but I also called out to my mom and my sister to assist God in protecting my daughter. They loved her so much, next to God I couldn't think of anyone else I'd rather act on my behalf.

Morgan had met our friend Tara out to dinner at the top of a mountain near a landmark known as the Pagoda in Reading, PA. There was a German restaurant Tara loved which the only option to and from are windy roads. It had started to rain very heavily that summer night and the clouds were blocking the light of the moon, making it very dark and difficult for Morgan to see. She navigated down the slippery mountain road in heavy rains with many hairpin turns that she had never driven before.

Morgan's Volvo began to spin out of control around a very sharp unexpected turn on the very dark, wet road. She said mom, the car was spinning and banging into the trees with such force and she was very close to a mountainside cliff. Morgan said it was weird how everything unfolded in slow motion. She was completely aware of every detail.

She added with all of the banging and spinning, she should have been thrashed about in the car like a rag doll. With the hit of each tree the car bounced like a ball making its way through a pinball machine. Morgan said she could feel she was being held down in place. Her entire body was held completely stable unmoved with every impact spinning from tree to tree. Like she was being held by an invisible force safely. She said she felt 3 women around her during this time. (My daughter also has intuitive gifts.)

I finally arrived to pick up Morgan and was so relieved to see her when she opened the door on this beautiful sunny day. I held her tightly appreciating having her in my arms. Morgan showed me where she was banged up on her chest and said she was sore. Once we got past the relief and happiness of seeing each other, Morgan informed me we needed to go sign over the title and pay the towing company so we wouldn't rack up anymore charges.

Morgan and I wanted to take a look at her car and also gather her belongings. I spotted Morgan's car when we rounded the top of the hill. My legs buckled underneath of me seeing Morgan's crumbled vehicle.

The Volvo was smashed in so badly on all sides except for Morgan's drivers side which seemed untouched. I looked in the passenger side door to check out the inside. My eye immediately went to a picture of my deceased sister Patti and Morgan from Morgan's first holy communion lying by itself. Morgan, what is that doing in your car??? It was like someone put it neatly right there on her passenger seat face up for us to see. When I asked Morgan what is this picture doing here? She said, I don't know I didn't put it there.

I picked up the picture and saw Morgan in her first holy communion gown and there was my sister standing behind her lovingly resting her hands on Morgan's shoulders, which looked like Patti had her hands on Morgan.......holding her in place. I felt omg, she is showing me, "I got her" with her hands holding Morgan's shoulders.

Morgan said she felt 3 women during the accident. We both felt my sister, my mom and my friend Tanya who was like a mother to her and only passed a month prior. Morgan wanted her mama as I suspected when this was all said and done. So we packed Morgan to go with me back to NJ so I could take care of her, let her just rest, feed her good food and just allow me love her up.

On the return to New Jersey, Morgan said her arms hurt. I said let me see honey, she showed me where it was hurting. I said oh you are bruised Mo that's why. I said wait, show me that again! I told Morgan it looked like a woman's finger prints on her arm. As if someone grabbed her arm. You could see 4 small finger print evenly spaced bruises. Thinking now of how Morgan told me she felt held down, and my sister's pic of her hands resting on Morgan's shoulders, now this. I feel like the invisible realm held on with all of their might.

There have been many moments of surrender in my lifetime, but never have I surrender more and completely. I felt the impending doom, I just felt and knew. I prayed with more than I ever have in my life. And never did I let go of my control with such commitment. I know this sounds crazy to know something bad is coming and the coincidence of the accident.

I initially didn't tell Morgan my feeling of she was going to die about 16 hours or so before the accident. Not until after I got her that day and she was safely in my arms and away from the situation. She mentioned earlier how she felt she was going to die and said she was actually surprisingly peaceful. The thing that came to Morgan's mind as she accepted the thought around death was me. She knew I would be devastated. She couldn't go she told me, she felt she needed to stay for me. She remembers having this whole conversation in her mind as her car was being tossed and spinning near the cliff side.

Had she never been in an accident, I would have never seen God's grace to us that day or learned about the power of letting God take control. Truly surrendering regardless of how much I wanted to control the happenings. I knew better. Morgan is one of my most treasured people in my lifetime. My girls are my heart and soul. I couldn't mess this up being egotistical thinking that I could do it best. There is a power far greater than any mama's love.

CHAPTER 13

We are all One

Have you ever heard this saying before, we are all one? What do you think about this concept? To me this was a grandiose thought at one point in my youth. I didn't quite grasp the idea. A little pollyanna-ish that we are all connected to each other in some way. Almost like a marketing catchphrase to rally some excitement. I first heard this in elementary school which is also where I was told I was being judged in every moment and learned to fear God. I felt like between Santa Claus and God there was a very long log being kept where you were categorized as "good" or "bad". No oneness, but rather an "either" "or" and very separate.

I later learned this idea of "we are all one" in a way that made sense to me in my spiritual studies. We are all energetically connected to God and each other, we all come from Source and all make up a part of the whole. We pull in the perfect match from the Universal Matrix where we are all connected. We attract our situations, from our focus, our prayers and beliefs, and the energy of where we are vibrationally. What we are presently attracting can change if we change our vibration and our focus.

Did you ever notice that there seems to be people you love to be around, that you naturally feel better in their presence? Have you met a joyful person seems to attract so much good in their lives? They hold a higher vibration and bring forth more of that high vibrational goodness. It seems they are a magnet for amazing opportunities and circumstances. Their higher vibe even expands into our energy affecting us seemingly leaving fairy dust in their trails! You are in a better mood after being with them.

Their good can influence your day in a positive way, then someone else's. And so on. The opposite can happen too, am I right?

I had a client who was the most adorable woman. But every time she came in to the salon for years it was the same routine every visit. There was a new story of some crazy hardship. Really unfortunate circumstances time after time. She went into elaborate detailed stories of which seemed entertaining to her and to all of us because it was done with a smile, humor, self-deprecation. She always ended her story with, "Well that's me and my luck." As a spiritual student I couldn't help but observe life around me and what people seemed to be attracting.

I clearly witnessed the effects in the power of your focus and words within myself and others. The story we tell feeds the energy we put out into the ethers and beliefs we are holding. So being all one.....you see where I am going? You are going to pull into your experience whatever's you speak or your area of focus. You could benefit to look at more closely and take responsibility for what you accept in your life, or where do you need to change in how you express yourself. By doing so, you can align better to experience love and support in your needs and desires! All depending on your focus in what you will receive from this Universal Matrix. Intended or unintended.

It seemed like a coincidence looking from the outside that I happened to be taken out to dinner to a Spanish restaurant after looking at houses all day because my when my boyfriend Norm had a Groupon. I ran into Kim, the Director of Education who I worked for 17 years prior as an educator. We were so happy to reconnect. Which is how I got my present job. My boss and I both felt that day was a fated crossing.

To me this was no coincidence. I was so very grateful as this day was the complete answer and manifestation of my intention. I had actually played the Wish around my intention and put out there prior to our running into each other. I asked, Universe can you please send to me my best job that I will love in New Jersey, where someone actually says....hey I heard of you. You are great you should come work for me. Seriously in a month the Universe delivered a match. It's been 5 years.

Since we affect the whole, wouldn't it be awesome work to on your vibe for yourself and the good of everyone? Believe it or not, we can raise each other just by being LOVE. Knowing I was moving to NJ and that I knew no one in that area, I called out for spiritually aligned and like minded friends who liked to have fun. We organically found each other through work and saw we were so alike in our spirit. A great group of cool, hip, funny, loving, deeply spiritually evolved women who are on a constant text thread. My spiritual sisters Sam, Susie, Tara, Kate, Bri and I laugh, support, process, and pray for each other daily. We often meet for wine and good food, or take spiritual classes when we can fit it in.

We are so supported more than we realize in our oneness. There is a flow, a harmony that may look chaotic to our human eye sometimes. But there is a beautiful mysterious dance of wisdom and perfection in everything.

No accidents my friend, just life syncing up in perfection. Bringing you what vibration you are sending out or by what you are setting things in motion with intention and prayers. We find the perfect people, the perfect circumstances. Whether it's for us to learn something, to grow, or enjoy!

Just a quick little add. There was a time I would have thought the Universal Matrix was not a thing. One time in my awakening I woke up one night to see a bright blue grid that looked like an airport runway glowing with lights that covered my hallway floor. It was a life size royal blue lights in a grid pattern that I noticed looked like a Matrix. I hadn't ever heard of an energetic matrix. I jumped over it and into the bathroom, lol. I have to admit I was a little freaked out. It scared me as many of new things I encountered did. I read the very next day in the book The Secret about the Universal Matrix. I said to myself,....OMG, THAT'S what that was? Wow. I began to see the matrix more and more in my vision and still do sometimes. It's a real thing guys! My daughter Morgan sees it in rainbow colors.

I have learned to think of life and the happenings as this gorgeous grand tapestry that is beautifully interwoven. Each thread when combined with the sum of its parts make up the whole. Each thread by itself doesn't make sense or is really all that impressive. But woven with the other threads purposefully in the grand design, it creates the most amazing picture. You see the beauty when you step back and look at the whole.

I find when we are going through something, we may not see the wisdom if we just look at the individual pieces or threads as we experience them. Like maybe losing a job that if you were completely honest maybe you were afraid to change. Maybe it provided an income but your boss was unreasonable, maybe it wasn't fulfilling or it had limited growth opportunities.

So maybe the Universe gives you a little nudge sometimes. When circumstance puts you in a better direction saying to you, ok you haven't been noticing my subtle inner promptings. Those moments are like the Universe is saying…..there is better waiting for you, here let me help you. Then comes a not so subtle push.

I have actually had a client who was let go from a company to move on to open her own business and she became a millionaire quickly. The moving parts came together by creating a direction she never would have considered had she not been terminated from her position. We may have no idea why things are happening while they are happening.

A woman I am friends with lost her job just short of retirement. Her ill husband's health took a turn for the worst about the time she was let go. Losing her job provided her the freedom and the opportunity to spend the last several months of her husband's life with her right by his side. She didn't know he was going to pass in about 6 months. She embraced every single day with the love of her life.

If you look at that singular thread at the time of being let go from her company, it's just a bad situation of her losing her job that seemed really heartless. It didn't take her long to see God's grace and wisdom in the whole beautiful tapestry.

Although the people at the company didn't know they were helping her, it was based on a business decision for the financial wellness of the company. Nonetheless there was a higher wisdom in perfect order that initially provoked fear that day my friend received her pink slip. Losing her job ended up being a beautiful gift of time devoted with laser focus on her husband. She wasn't a victim, it was God's grace and Universal wisdom.

The following is a story that showed me there is a higher wisdom and perfection in the orchestration. I learned in time how everyone was blessed, how prayers were heard and answered. As well as how we are connected and things perfectly came together with blessings for everyone. We may not always know our role in how we may affect each other. The perfect fit of the puzzle pieces always play into the vibration of each other's lessons, growth or needs and desires so perfectly.

And THEN the phone rang!

This story goes all the way back to me being pregnant with Jadin and wanting to get our basement finished. There would be an almost 6 year difference between Morgan and Jadin. At 5 years old, Morgan was an extremely high energy little girl used to making lots and lots of noise. I wanted to maintain Morgan's play dates, keeping things as routine for her as possible. I am sure you can imagine how it can be while being outnumbered by several 5 year olds at our playdates. It wasn't exactly be a recipe for quiet or keeping the noise to a low roar.

What springs to mind is remembering the happy squeals in the house with Morgan and her friends had by being together. If I could separate that noisy enthusiasm to another floor while working on the little hours of sleep with a newborn, well that would be a slice of heaven. Everyone wins. Morgan would have freedom to continue to enjoy her friends and I would have peace while the mess would be kept out of eyesight behind a closed door to the basement. All while Jadin could sleep (Jadin and I both win with that one.)

At this point I was pretty good at putting out to the angels my requests for guidance and hearing their communication. When I say hearing, I am not speaking always audibly. Often it's more of a feeling inside that comes by being present, checking with in my body. Trusting the vibe you feel and being directed in a 'knowing" for me is mostly what I recognize. Hearing may even come in the form of getting an inspired idea. The more I meditate I find it easier to hear actual words as guidance in my mind. When I hear guidance it is simple, direct, never negative. Which my self talk isn't always loving. Guidance is always loving, direct, and not wordy.

I had put out a request to the Universe, "please send me someone to finish our basement that was in our budget and who would do a fantastic job for us." I also asked that God and the angels, "please send a person who we love having in our home, that we are a blessing to him as well as he is a blessing to us." And also added as Nancy instructed me to do because why not? "Please bring the right person to me."

It was about a week when I overheard a client in my salon getting her hair done telling her stylist about her wonderful neighbor who does work for her at her home. He is reasonable and does a great job. I joined in the conversation, excited to hear more about this person. I learned he was a retired contractor who built houses, and a really nice man to boot she added. I asked her if he is ever interested in taking on jobs for other people or is it just for her? She thought that he may be open to certain jobs and to give him a call. I left that day with Ron's phone number scrolled on a piece of scrap paper tucked in my pocket.

I didn't understand just yet, and really didn't ever expect to find out why things unfolded the way they did. I did understand already that we are all connected and timings of things, that there were no accidents in how we played a role in each other's lives. When I felt God was behind something, I listened obediently. Who am I to question, although there are times I still do.

I picked up the phone to call Ron and something stopped me dead in my tracks. I heard, "not yet, not today." I just felt curious, but it's not mine to know. I honor when it's clear I am being led with a higher direction, when I know it's not coming from myself. I didn't ask if it was a good time when I first picked up the phone. I only had the simple intention of making that call, but that voice that I recognized as God or guidance was *clearly* speaking to me. I put the phone down and said to myself, ok I guess I am not supposed to call today. I made us dinner, gave Morgan a bath and got ready for bed, and called it a night.

Picking up the phone to call Ron again went on about 2 more times. I heard again "nope, not today." Eventually I just asked before I even picked up the phone, what about today should I call today? "Nope, not yet," I would hear again. Until one day I felt with urgency, "Call him NOW!" I didn't listen to the direction at that moment so I heard again, "RIGHT NOW." I had started to finish putting the laundry away and figured in a minute I will get to calling after I had my chores finished. Suddenly and urgently I felt like I was very strongly being pushed to *put that laundry down*. I then said out loud, "OK, I hear you, right now!" I completely stopped walking in the direction I was headed, turned around and went immediately to the phone in my kitchen.

I introduced myself to Ron on the phone that day, it was about dinner time and apologized for interrupting his dinner. I told him how I heard of him and was wondering if he would consider finishing our basement. There was a pause and silence for a second, he then said yes he would. He told me what he charged and it seemed so reasonable. Ron only charged by the hour, he explained he would tell us what to order from Lowe's and we would have it delivered. Most contractors charge at least double or triple for materials. When he informed me that we would only pay our cost for materials and his hourly rate, it was looking hopeful for us.

We met Ron for the first time when he arrived at our house to look at our basement and consult around our design. He is a true Pennsylvania Dutch older gentleman complete with the Pennsylvania Dutch accent. Just the sweetest soft spoken gentle person, but manly at the same time. We walked around the basement together while I told him how many closets I hoped to have, where the family area would be. Basically we custom designed everything and he told me how he could make it work. I was so blown away that his estimate for the our best vision was totally with in our budget. He said he could get started first thing Monday.

That weekend I began to get some very strong contractions that stopped my dead in my tracks. I ended up on bedrest while about 6 months pregnant with Jadin in danger of losing her. I was a bit lonely by myself. I was used to being around people all day doing hair.

Because I couldn't work and had to get off of my feet I got to know this adorable man who did such a lovely job on our basement.

I felt better physically when I laid down most of the time, if I got up for more than a few minutes I would go into full and steady contractions. I tried to do a few things like lift a laundry basket or tidy up the clutter laying around. It would result in awful pain by bedtime and with really strong contractions for hours. I learned after a bit to just get up for food or a snack and get back to resting.

I told Ron if I had to get up to make myself lunch why don't I just make him lunch as well. It's not really any more effort to do two lunches if I was already doing one. I really enjoyed when I would yell down to Ron, are you ready for lunch? He would come up to the kitchen and sit at the table with me, we would have a nice chat together and then he would return to working downstairs when he finished eating. He told me his wife would ask about me, because I guess other people typically don't feed the work men. After dedicated years of making his daily lunch, his wife didn't need to pack him lunch for his time at our house.

My mom taught us well with that too. No matter who came to fix something, paint something, the lawn, they were always fed and treated with respect and kindness. It was factored into our grocery shopping for the week if we knew anyone was going to be working on our home. My mom would put me to work asking them what kind of sandwich they wanted, complete with chips and freshly baked cake made by my mom, served to them at our table with sodas or my mom's fresh batch of sweet tea.

So after a few weeks our basement was finished, it looked wonderful! I had a huge 11 foot wide by 3 feet deep closet to just store all of the girls toys. I mean I could put away the play kitchens, barbie houses and cars, board games and bins on shelves you name it … it fit in the closet. Nice living area, about 1000 square feet finished with lots of storage.

I recommended Ron to so many friends and neighbors, he had work for many months to come. I think he landed at least 8 jobs from me. Who knows how many more opportunities came to him from those new jobs he had gotten. No accident I believed. I had my prayer answered with someone I loved working in my home, reasonably priced, and beautiful quality work. I was surprised one day when I found out a something very special about a certain thread in our grand tapestry I had no idea about. What I was told next I learned a special detail about God's amazing wisdom. How His grand design is beyond what we could ever create.

A few months after our basement was finished I had a conversation while waiting for the school bus with a woman who lived across the street. My neighbor Chris hired Ron to finish her basement. I had sung his praises to all the neighbors at a block party and welcomed people to come look at his work. This day at the bus stop Chris said jokingly to me, "thanks a lot Donna." I had no idea what she was talking about. Chris shared that now SHE had to make Ron lunch every day because he made a big fuss about me having lunch for him everyday while he did work to my house.

What Chris told me next I never saw coming. Remember how I asked God to please send me a person who I would love to have in my home who we could afford, that we are blessing to them as well they are a blessing to us? And how I kept hearing no, don't call yet. Nope, not yet. Then I heard NOW call NOW. Ron told Chris that he and his wife were on their last few dollars. It looked like they were enjoying one of their last meals. They didn't know how they would survive, as Ron had no more jobs lined up. Being a family of faith, they were at the dinner table praying over their meal hand in hand. They prayed for God to please send Ron work, something, anything….. they desperately needed money. They didn't know what to do.

They were still holding hands praying together when the phone rang. Ron answered the phone, hello? It was me! I asked Ron if he would consider finishing my basement. The pause before he answered me was the shock of the timing, God's right on time....every time. That's why I kept hearing to wait every time I went to pick up the phone. Ron was not only an answer to my prayers, WE were also the answer to HIS prayers. And the answer to Ron's prayers was impactful due to the timing of my call. We never know why we may feel a certain way, is it guidance? I didn't know why at the moment, but I found out months later I was a part of the plan for Ron and Ron was a part of mine. We are all connected, it's all perfect. And even better when we live with awareness, miracles await and it's so much fun!

The Universe Knows Your Greatest Wish

My initial interest in being trained on how to properly facilitate the Wish was to help people during one on one in a coaching sessions in the most beneficial way. I hadn't thought beyond coaching one person at a time.

There was a description on the Wish website for the training that I didn't quite understand. The ad mentioned we would be learning how to take the Wish into our community. I thought why would I take this into the community? Louise and her teachers explained during our training in Florida how you can do group events. I was excited to hear that we were already being featured at the Deepak Chopra Center having been played with 300 people at the same time.

I was informed of how it can be used in a business environment or for corporate team building. It can also be used in goal setting one on one or even executive strategy meetings. That really lit a fire within me. With my dad being a very successful business owner, I grew up in a house where discussions of business strategies, growth potential, profit and loss statements and customer service were nightly dinner table discussions. I had a business root in my foundation, but a creative soul.

I quickly got comfortable with doing games one on one and the feedback was that my clients loved our sessions. I kept hearing my guidance tell me

I could be helping *more* people than one-on-one. I started to feel called to do group events. That inner voice kept at me until I listened and got on board, it's time to do a group event.

I decided to ask Spirit, "ok where do I start?" I immediately heard, "call Thrive Yoga Center." I ignored my inner promptings a few times…..you know how we do that at times. I realized my procrastination was that I had a bit of self-doubt. "Can I do this?" I asked myself. "What makes me think I can do that?" But the inner prompting kept coming.

So I decided one day to take my step, have some courage and call Sue, the owner of Thrive Yoga. I had attended an Archangel Michael class at Thrive Yoga and met Sue briefly. I really liked who Sue was as a person and hoped she remembered me. I was greeted with immediate enthusiasm over the phone. She had remembered me when I explained who I was.

I described to Sue what I would be offering as an event with my Wish games, what it was about. We had a quick but lovely little chat and booked a time to meet for Sue to experience firsthand the intricacies of the game. Sue really liked what she experienced so a date was booked! And there it was…. my very first Wish Event!

Sue marketed to her client base, and me to my clients and friends. Even thought it was about an hour from my area, I had so many people show that I invited. Sue also had a fantastic turnout from her clientele as well. We had about 30 people my first event! Everyone showed with such excitement and wanting to learn about this manifesting game. I walked around intuitively being drawn to a person at this or that table as Louise and her teachers taught us, to assist someone who needed help in shifting their energy.

The key to empowering someone to shift is not to tell them what "I" think, but rather guide them to their own deeper wisdom and how they are relating to a statement. To someplace where you may feel this thought originated, is it truth? Is it someone else's thought and beliefs that was imposed upon you intentionally or unintentionally? And where is your truth around this statement? What do you feel? Then I ask, how does this statement relate to your wish?

However, sometimes I share what I feel a message may be. I tell the attendees what myself or others will share during the game will either resonate you or it will not. But either way it's a clue to how you feel around what is said to you, bringing you more insight. Epiphanies had during the game result in energetic shifts and you often can feel in your body.

I became a regular at Thrive Yoga and word spread in through the spiritual community. I had many people emailing me or approaching me at future events about how they had their wish come true, some with receiving large amounts of money, some with saved marriages, re-established relationships with family members soon after their wish with relatives who wouldn't give them the time of day. Some players had a wish around having their own businesses that quickly came true. Many doors opened for me without trying to do more events at a few other Holistic centers who heard about me and my fantastic game.

I had been feeling pretty good about the flow of doing an events, and saw how these events were spreading joy, bringing peace and empowering people. People were being helped quickly in seeing how they may have been getting in their own way without realizing it. It came to me one day, I am ready. I want to do a corporate event.

Well THAT was fast!

My biggest goal in doing business events was to do an executive strategy meeting for a Fortune 500 company. But my mind said, well you have to start small and get experience. You must crawl before you walk kind of thinking. So one day I decided to put out there, "Universe please bring to me an opportunity to facilitate corporate Wish game." "That I would enjoy the experience and the business would enjoy me and our time together." "That we benefit by being together, I ask that it come to me soon." Again as with many of my requests, I didn't give it a second thought, I completely let it go.

Three days later, one of my favorite clients Amy was scheduled with me to get highlights and a haircut. I always looked forward to our time together at her appointments. Amy embodies what a connected and conscious life looks like. Totally choosing to think positive, allowing what comes with grace and goes with the flow. She possesses a great sense of self-worth. Good always seems to unfold for her magically. She is the vibe that breathes and attracts goodness.

Amy and I always had the most fun and lively conversations, humorous outlooks on life. We chatted about her life happenings for the first part of the visit. At one point Amy asked me to tell her about my spiritual work, asking me what's new? And what is this Wish she had been seeing more on my facebook page, she asked.

I explained deeper around what the Wish is and how it works. I felt guided to add, "we even do corporate Wish events for team building, goal setting, and executive strategy meetings." The Wish was played in government and corporate settings worldwide. I just had never done one, hence the "we."

Amy was the head of human resources for a Fortune 500 company, she even had the honor to ring the opening bell one morning on the New York Stock Market Exchange. She stated her company was always looking for more team building ideas and asked if I had any information she could forward to the person making the decisions. This moment unfolded just as I had asked.

One of things I forgot to mention I stated in my request to the Universe was that I don't want to bother anyone with this, I have many business clients. I respect and honor that they are coming to me for hair and this is their "me" time, to get a little pampering and let go for a while. I wanted this wish around doing a corporate event to come to me in love and unfold organically without pushing my goals and making people uncomfortable. My request that someone ask me about appearing at a business wish was made only 3 days prior to Amy asking. That was quick! Which by the way.....one of the meanings of 3 in Wish numerology is LIFE PURPOSE.

I reached out to Louise in Australia and she was elated with the news. Louise was so incredibly supportive, she forwarded me a PDF of an article about how the results of playing the Wish affects our brain patterning and neural pathways into new habitual patterns of thought. It was several weeks later, I received a call from Amy to inquire how much I would charge. Again calling Louise in Australia, where do I even begin? I didn't want to outbid my opportunity, nor did I want to undermine myself for my special knowledge and many years of study and investment.

Another few weeks passed and I got the news. I was chosen to do a Wish Event at the Fortune 500 Company, and asked to appear at their National Executive Strategy Meeting in NYC. Top executives from every department from all over the United States. Ok, first.....EXECUTIVE STRATEGY MEETING?? That was enough. Then I found out the FBI was going to go on before me, I forget the topic, something along the lines of interviewing and reading people's body language and cues. I laughed at myself, ok the FBI and ME! A hairdresser who never did anything like this *but just felt capable and made a wish*....and the FBI.

Well I felt capable until I found out it was in NYC, then I felt very uncomfortable. I am NOT a city girl, and get lost very easily. As my fears mounted, I told myself Ok Criqui you created this....maybe you can create something different. Their headquarters were only about 40 minutes from my home. Why wasn't it there?

I asked the Universe, is there any way for this event to be moved? I put my request out saying..... thank you for this amazing opportunity however, I would be more comfortable if it were not in the city. Please I am asking for the highest good of all that the conference is moved. I accepted within myself that if it really was to be in NYC that it would be exciting. And maybe I was supposed to learn how to have courage and navigate a city better. Maybe I am to stretch beyond my self-imposed limitations to more. I let my agenda go to the higher wisdom of the Universe.

A few weeks before the event I was told by Amy via email, it's no longer in New York City. They decided to move the conference to the corporate headquarters the same date, now only 40 minutes from my home.

When I arrived to the Corporate Headquarters the meeting was already in session. They were about a few hours in and different presenters had completed their trainings. I had the opportunity to observe the group before I took center stage. The Executives were sitting at the biggest and longest conference table I had ever seen in my life, it seemed to go on forever. The vibe of the meeting was VERY serious and professional.

I asked Amy if all the sessions they had been having were of this intense nature. Which she responded, yes. I thought it would benefit the executives to be in a lighter and relaxed state than their serious present demeanor. To somehow shift to the creative side of their brain.....outside of the logic and reasoning side which is where they just spent their entire day. I couldn't help but notice the beautiful adjoining open airy room with so many different colorful designs, funky and artsy tables and chairs. Totally fun and playful vibe!

So I asked if we could possibly shift gears and maybe have the everyone stand up and move to this fun colorful space away from the serious energy when it came for our time together. Amy said that sure that would be fine. So I set up the games quietly where they could play and share ideas with each other in the adjoining room and discover more about themselves.

Right before I went on, Amy informed me that she had no influence in me being picked. That my submission was shuffled in with the many other potential presenters. Amy never spoke of her affiliation with me.

It was the President of the Fortune 500 Company who picked me to be one of the presenters based on the information I compiled and the articles about the Wish. I must admit, prior to Amy sharing this information with me I felt a bit of ....well is this really a manifestation....because I know Amy.

That information that no one knew we knew each other was wonderful information to be given before I took center stage.

When it was my turn they announced my name and I walked before this elite group of executives. There I stood looking down this long table with the full attention of top people nationally in their prospective departments looking to me at the head of the table.... all eyes and ears totally engaged and captive.

I took in this moment to look around the room listening to the sound of my own voice speaking, smiles being reflected back to me....OMG I AM HERE! THIS IS HAPPENING !?! I felt like my body was floating realizing a dream of mine is this happening right NOW. I snapped out of my little surreal actualization and continued with my presentation.

Everyone was very cooperative about picking up and moving to the next room. I began by making this fun to help loosen the executives up and shift gears. I had found online stories of Lucille Ball, Michael Jordan, Thomas Edison and Walt Disney of how they each were told they didn't have what it takes to pursue their dreams. We all know they were huge successes and are legends to us all.

These historical icons were an example of how to be in tune with who you are and not to allow others define you, to be in your own integrity and be authentic to yourself. My intent was to set the tone prior to the game to explain the power of our minds and our beliefs have on our success.

I posed the questions as a verbal quiz to the group once we moved to the funky room, with them sitting around the many Wish games. THIS ACTRESS/COMEDIAN in the 1920's at 15 YEARS OLD WENT TO A DRAMA SCHOOL. THE SCHOOL SENT HER HOME SAYING SHE WAS WASTING THEIR TIME AND HERS. SAYING THAT SHE HAD NO TALENT AFTER ONLY ONE WEEK. SHE WENT ONTO HAVE HER OWN TV SHOW, SHE BEGAN AS A MODEL.... A few guesses were made...I gave another clue..... SHE HAD RED HAIR. Of course that story was Lucille Ball, the red hair gave it away.

I continued my fun quiz trying to guess the other icons. My point in the exercise was to demonstrate just because someone says something against us, our talents, and who we are as a person, does this make it true? People can make us doubt ourselves or how life's little stumbling blocks can mean the end if we allow it to be the end. All of these icons had in common a strong sense of self, an inner drive and dedicated to themselves and their passion. They all kept that spark of self-worth and their dreams alive. Had they not been clear on their desires, their higher truth, and allowed others rejection to influence them, they would have had very different results.

Something very special about the wish is it is a game of the highest vibration, which is love. Which is of the highest and most beautiful vibration in the Universe. The game creates an air of cooperation among the players. The blue color of the wish silk which is our playing surface or game board, clears any negativity. I have seen this game really open people to good behavior and helpfulness.

As I walked around to help people, I observed enthusiasm and care. Previously competitive people who were put together purposely were genuinely saying kind and supportive things about each other when a person was stuck for an answer. They were generously sharing about the other person's strengths while vulnerability was shared in their own perceived limitations.

This time together enabled everyone see a deeper and more compassionate side of each other. For some that had previously erected a wall not letting others in, now was being exchanged for an air of openness and cooperation. Seeing each other through a new softened lens was a benefit from this day of discovery together.

I intended to keep the Wish strictly as a coaching tool since this was a professional environment. I didn't talk about it on a spiritual level. There is much more to the game such as sacred geometry, the number patterns that show up, such as if you keep rolling 4's and 2's. People at the same table kept picking the same card out of over 400 cards. Some of the participants were flying through the game and while others were stuck. People couldn't help but notice some of the patterns and began to ask me questions. Hey Donna we keep picking the same card out of over 400 cards. Why is that?

I fessed up there is a deeper level to this game if they were open to it. I explained what they witnessing really is a clue to the energy they are holding and a message is being revealed. Next thing I knew I was running from one side of the room to the other revealing the messages around the insights people were having. Donna I keep rolling 3's what does that mean? Why does he have 7 pearls of wisdom and I can't keep seem to keep any?

One time at one of my Yoga Studio events a woman made a professional wish to get promoted. She informed me she always seems to get passed over when there was an opportunity at her company. She picked the Rose Quartz as her playing piece when she reached into the bag containing the crystals with her eyes closed.

This woman looked at her Rose Quartz meaning on the card which was all about LOVE.

She called me over and said, I don't get this. I asked about work and this is all about LOVE! She was a bit angry about it. I said maybe that is a message for you, let's sit deeper around this. I asked her if is it possible this is a message about self love? What are your thoughts about yourself, how do you feel when I ask you if you love yourself? She immediately began to cry.

I helped her understand self love this is exactly what she needs to help herself get promoted. It was at the root of what has been holding her back. What is showing up professionally will change when you love yourself and value yourself. You are more confident in who you are, and accept nothing less than what is good for you, including how *you treat yourself.* When you start loving and valuing yourself others will as well, even professionally. Let's start here. She saw the wisdom of the messages revealed in the game, better thoughts and truths were unveiled for her.

The feedback from the game at my Fortune 500 game was that it was memorable and everyone really loved the experience, and they would like to do it again. I did get some honest feedback from Amy that when I gave the directions part it was a bit confusing. I knew exactly where she said and I agreed. At one point I got wobbly as I gave the directions. It was a group of leaders who were used to directing their staff and were ambitious in getting moving. I wanted to please the group and ran helping from person to person instead of commanding quiet and focus and all eyes and ears on me. I needed to shift to the leader and be centered in that role for the moment and not the polite people pleaser.

Funny how now I teach big groups now and have been on stage as a featured artist because of my job with my beauty company. But I feel that I have evolved in that role of getting control of the group and there was no accident I have been put in situations to grow. Always something to learn and we are always led to where we need to be.

Louise and I had a call scheduled for afterwards for me to fill her in on my day and her game being played in the USA at a Fortune 500 company! I only wished to do a corporate wish I told Louise. My ULTIMATE end goal was a Fortune 500 Executive Strategy meeting. I didn't even wish that big, I thought I had to start small and work my way up to it. Louise said to me, "the Universe knows your greatest wish!"

We are all one in the Universe. So when I aligned with my wish I attracted the perfect fit for my current vibe. I sincerely put my deepest intention out there and being unattached in faith for what would show for me up. Which what I got was really my bucket list experience wish! Start your unfolding by asking, and trust in the whole grand design my friends and gifts the Universe wishes to give you. It may come as better and more than you are even hoping!

CHAPTER 14

Managing Your Energy

Before I begin explaining about managing your energy I would like to address a very important point. I honor the wisdom of the Universe, of God and the higher plan. Timing is 100% God's timing. Yes I've read what I wrote about the law of attraction, lol. Yes to all of it, but we really don't have the final say. Life is our earth classroom and *if it is given it is required.* Meaning there are no mistakes in us experiencing something we don't love. That there is something valuable in every situation we face that would benefit us if we observed what the Universe is trying to help us with what we need to see. Life refines and shapes us through our experiences.

Energetically speaking, there are moments we may get in the way to the possibilities. By managing our energy which is accomplished with awareness and focus around our perceptions, beliefs, thoughts, feelings and emotions - we can influence the trajectory of what we will experiences in our lives. We can create some beautiful things being a co-creator with the Universe ~ all while simultaneously honoring the highest wisdom. Remember when chapters back I stopped complaining and being negative and the world around me became more positive? Life became more enjoyable.

When I speak of managing your energy, I am speaking about being intentionally and consciously responsible for your energy. To have awareness of where your mind dwells, how you feel in your emotions, in your body, the words you are speaking, and empowering your mind with beautiful and empowering or inspiring thoughts. To observe the energy of what is showing up for you in your experiences and to be aware of what may serve you to let go of from the past. I know this may sound like a lot if you are new to this concept.

When we are in our *conscious self,* we are empowering ourselves from the inside out. We choose from the inside where we wish to place our focus and the energy. Energy comes from within us and travels out to the Universe. We purposely choose from a higher awareness where we wish to be in our thoughts and energy even when the outside doesn't look or feel so great. The outside responds to our intention and our energy.

Conversely being unconscious or *self-conscious* is where we feel victimized in our experiences. It feels like life is coming at us, happening to us. We allow circumstances to control our moods and how we react. Here is where we can shift, when we see we are reacting to circumstances and feeling like life is coming at us. You now will instead go within to manage your energy where you decide how you will be in your energy! Best place to begin is in your heart space. What is your heart saying from an evolved place? How do you wish to be? The wisdom is within.

Trust me when I say if you make this an everyday practice it becomes easier and easier. And seeing the shift in your experiences are motivating to continue. As we begin to heal and feel lighter and freer in our energy, we open the door to fresh opportunities and ways of being that feel pretty amazing within ourselves. When we choose to be in the higher vibrations such as love, joy, gratitude, enjoying life and having fun, you have stepped into your natural alignment and in flow.

You can choose to let go of what you learned in the past, it doesn't matter what anybody else did, or what your parents said or how anyone acted, it now becomes about awareness of the present and how you choose to respond and be in each moment. If you change the habits of what you have been holding mentally, emotionally and therefore energetically and you instead go within and align with better thoughts, practices, and habits - you now empower yourself to change your experiences. From this enlightened aspect of yourself you align with a life that feels better and attracts better while we trust in God's higher plan and timing.

I love listening to comedy stations on Sirius Radio as I drive. It's how I can make my long rides in the car fun. I heard a comedian say yesterday, show of hands who addresses God as "the Nemesis?" I laughed, I am sure we all have wondered at times if God was against us or had a sick sense of humor with how life can feel at times.

Remember that life is happening FOR you to bring you more in alignment with LOVE energy. It benefits us to work WITH the energy presenting itself in your experiences. Get your mind empowered and motivated to take some inspired action of how to choose better and cultivate more evolved and higher thoughts all while embracing yourself with healthy doses of radical self love.

Energy Tip:

It serves you to remember to be centered in your heart space, to feel the energy within your body, and be in the present moment fully, which puts you in the natural flow of the universe.

What can flow feel like?

To me being connected in a great flow of energy is like riding a nice sized wave in the ocean and letting it playfully take you on an exhilarating ride. Or naturally feeling into the rhythm of the music and effortlessly following your dance partner when you are completely in sync with each other. It feels so great because it just works so easily when you are tapped into the beauty of the moment. You feel the unseen connection with your partner when you let go to the moment. There is no forcing, it's natural and joyful. You know what direction to go next in your dance because you are tapped into the subtle cues of your partner. Except the partner energetically is THE UNIVERSE.

Relax more, Breathe easy, and celebrate little moments ~

Can you imagine the possibilities of what you would experience if your habits became aligned with having a positive lens to look through? Celebrating life's little successes as they come along, adding in a little loving self-talk into your day? It is a discipline and a practice.

Imagine if you shared your love openly with others and celebrated the love that exists in your life by expressing it authentically with others, if you took moments to nurture your soul, released your fears, remained hopeful and open to new ideas for yourself without limits. Saying yes to life. And always celebrating and loving yourself for just being YOU.

How do you see? ~

Our thoughts and our filter or the lens through which we perceive life are kind of habits aren't they? The way we think and feel for most of us really can be pretty much the same day in and day out. YOU have the creative power and the authority to change the way you choose to see things. This wisdom was summarized profoundly by Wayne Dyer, *"When you change the way you look at things, the things you look at change."*

In my friend Sherry's situation, it wasn't about telling herself she was happy and being positive in her abusive relationship, not at ALL! It was about loving herself enough to shift from her perception of being stuck and hopeless in her situation. She was stuck in her mind by dwelling in her thoughts around being a victim in her situation. Changes began to happen for Sherry when she became clear in her vision around her desires for her life.

From there she shifted to more empowering ways of thinking such as, I do not deserve this treatment, how do I get out?

Sherry's prayers became God help me to see what I need to see, show me how we will be safe and ok financially. Empowering the energy in her daily was because she changed her focus to solutions, and she also visualized daily playing with her children with the feeling of joy and freedom helped her to feel amazing.

Even the smallest change puts things in motion:

What if you took the time to _see the little nice happenings throughout your day_? Maybe finally someone gave you a break and let you in traffic where no one else was letting you in. Or you got a phone call from an old friend out of the blue and how you felt so happy in that moment. Remembering the compliment you got on your efforts at work, that was really nice. Or the fact that your meeting was cancelled which gave you the extra time to get things done that really needed your attention. Appreciate those little happenings.

Tell the Universe thank you as you see these little blessings. Didn't these wonderful little gifts actually make your day a bit nicer in that moment? Yes, you may have had the grumbly person who annoyed you. Let it roll off you like water off a duck's back. Don't let THAT person's yuk be your focus and take off track of the good energy flow going on. Hop back on that love train and stay free of judging yourself from falling off in the first place. Instead say you got this, good job for seeing and choosing better. Hurray for you! You know what gratitude for all of these little gifts brings more of? More gifts!

Feed the beauty of this moment with your full attention. With people you enjoy, doing activities you enjoy, even being fully present at work. This is all contributing to creating a greater and higher vibration by being in the present. Why? Well your mind isn't dwelling in the past or the future. Many times if we think about the past we think about the past with regret, guilt or criticism. If we are thinking of the future is usually worrying about the what' ifs and the stories we create in our minds. Being present and feeling into the moment from your heart allows God's natural flow. Wouldn't you love to create from here? From the wonderful vibration of being in flow with God? Remember Soldraham's message to me when I was trying to conceive - Be one with God. Be present.

Changing habits to better ~

Now how do we change our filter? Well with some practice. You begin to create new habits when you catch yourself feeling off or negative. Instead of feeding the negative, choose to take your mind into a better place with your attention and rise above and beyond those habits of where you go by habit go to in your mind.

For example, just today I really took notice of how beautiful the Walt Whitman Bridge is while driving into Philadelphia to teach an advanced color class. I noticed the bridge not by choice, I hit super heavy traffic during the early morning rush hour. I could have started feeding my initial reaction of being annoyed and complain with a statement such as; well isn't this just lovely....I am going to be late for my class! I could have let that feeling really start a mood that carried with me throughout my day. But I knew I had a choice.

I decided as I saw the wall of cars in front of me, you can't control the traffic, right Donna? I thought, well Universe I guess this is how you want things to be right now for whatever reason. This could be saving me from an accident, who knows why the delay from a higher perspective. Instead I took advantage of this slow time suspended several hundreds of feet stuck over the water.

I decided instead to be present and take a look at what I could notice in that moment. I saw the most gorgeous sunbeams coming through the clouds and into my car. That felt so soothing actually, and that led me to feeling into my God connection. And because I was really not moving, it gave me opportunity to really check out the details of the bridge that I drive over all the time and have never really truly noticed.

The Walt Whitman Bridge arches are so immensely tall. As I gazed upward the sky was so blue against the color of the green arches. I never noticed the color of the bridge before. I thought the arches were blue! I began to wonder who was brave enough to be up there working on this gigantic project as it was built so many years ago. What about the brilliant minds of the engineers who created the design for the millions of cars have crossed from NJ to PA.

I usually speed through so fast I just have to watch the traffic. But today I saw new beauty in something I never noticed. Instead of feeding my initial thought I am late and I really fear being stuck suspended so high over the water on a bridge. You see where I am going? We choose the focus!

Whatever you are looking for.....you will find. What if you looked at something with a *curiosity* instead of judgement? What if you choose a positive lens versus traveling down the path of putting yourself into a bad mood by dwelling on what you see as upsetting.

And fast forward to reviewing my day, we had a gorgeous class. Great attitudes, we really enjoyed each other's company and positive interactions, we loved our creative color project and the end result of our hair color model was gorgeous!! What if I showed up annoyed and anxious and that was the energy of what brought into my class? It ripples into others and into my day, right?

Manage your energy, your environment responds. We often assume things are working against us when truly we just have to look with in. We decide how to respond every moment.

> **"You've always had the power my dear, you just had to learn it for yourself."**
> **~Glenda the Good Witch, Wizard of OZ**

Daily practice of your new awareness and focus

Think of managing your energy like you would if you decided to improve your physical body. When you want to improve your physical body, you incorporate better habits into your lifestyle of eating better and become committed to exercising more. When you begin to make positive changes in your diet and more exercise you suddenly are aware of your activity and everything you eat. After time you can visibly see the positive changes in your body and you notice you feel better. **Effort + consistency = results.**

When you are dedicated to your daily **spiritual health and the energy of love, and begin to love yourself** you will see a change in the world around you by tending to your *self*, your energy and spirit. **Effort + consistency = results**. Very much like when you discipline yourself when dedicate yourself to exercise. You will absolutely see the results of your better and higher focus in the world around you. Suddenly you notice things are going more smoothly, you feel more relaxed and more adaptable. Next thing you know things begin to shift in your world as well.

If you slip back to old habits of complaining, being a victim, life happening TO you, just recognize it and know you can choose again. Be easy with yourself, it is so worth the effort to try new ways of being. We have a card in the Wish game that I absolutely love, *"If you keep doing what you've been doing, you are going to get where you've been going."*

BEING ~ stillness

Beyond thinking from an evolved way of navigating life from "doing" or taking action, you can be more effective when you decide to just BE. Yes it sounds so crazy doesn't it? We often feel we have to do *something*. BEing is very freeing. BEing is often necessary! Absence of thoughts in our minds. What if you just relaxed for a while. Stop the obsessing and the need to DO anything and just BE still. Literally. Relax your body and slowly breathe in taking deliberate deep slow breaths in and out. Disconnect and take a break from the ranting mind, just tell it to take a rest for a moment, let your mind and body be quiet and still. A world of wisdom and lighter will unfolds for you. BEing present puts us in flow and allows the Universe to bring to us the gifts it wishes to deliver when we are in a state of allowing or non-resistance. Simply BE.

> **"I think 99 times and I find nothing. I stop thinking, swim in silence, and the truth comes to me." ~ Albert Einstein**

Being can even look like being present while relaxing on a park bench, a day of vegging and recharging watching Netflix under a blanket just being quiet. Tending to whatever it is your spirit is craving to recharge your soul. You will be so glad you are beginning to listen!

Embodying the energy you desire to receive ~

We talked a lot about you and how to manage YOUR energy. Mainly because it is so important to have love for ourselves and take responsibility for what we are vibrating energetically. From this loved space we see more clearly, and operate from a better place, and can give from a heart centered and loving space.

So what if we looked beyond ourselves and took our focus to the present needs of seeing how others are doing? What if we looked to be the energy of how you wish to receive treatment? Remember the golden rule from kindergarten? *Treat others as you wish to be treated.* It's so simple. This rule creates a beautiful harmony and oneness doesn't it?

Respect others, act with kindness and generosity. Energetically It has no choice but to come back to you in the most gorgeous ways and sometimes in ways you would not expect. And it may not be in the moment you decide to be generous. It may surprise you in the most beautiful ways in the future! When you spread love it creates a higher vibration in the world by doing so! We are not here to be in existence alone, we can enhance each other's journey of life. Let's work together to take care of each other.

BE THE CHANGE YOU WISH TO SEE IN THE WORLD ~
Mahatma Gandhi

Be kind just to be kind. YOU let that person in traffic who needs a break, when someone isn't kind to you - take a deep breath and maybe you extend the olive branch seeing that person maybe having a bad day. Maybe hand someone a few dollars or anonymously leave them a gift card for food or a clothing store if you know they are having a tough time financially. Maybe they could use it to lighten their burden and allow them some peace and it would help them to feel loved and understood. Take the time to listen to someone when it seems like they could really use an ear, even in the most unlikely places, even if you don't know them, even if you have 1000 things waiting for you to do.

It's interesting how giving always comes back, maybe not in the moment. But remember everything is energy. BE and embody how you would love to be treated yourself, and BE THAT. Is it with respect, love, humor, lighthearted, engaging, full attention, dedication, cooperation, helpful, generosity, supportive? Act with your best towards others. Put out what you would like to receive without expectation from another. Just give with love. Have fun observing what you have been putting out and see what you receive.

I was discussing this concept of how energy comes back to us with my daughter Morgan's boyfriend Kevin. He is in his early 20's and such a great spirit. He was agreeing with me and gave me an example where he experienced this first hand.

A few years ago Kevin was down to his last $20 and was going to use it for food one day and went to grab a bite at the mini-mart. He encountered a stranger who expressed such panic in the need for money for gas to get home. So Kevin handed this stranger everything he had until his next paycheck. Kevin said he thought to himself, I will get food somehow and didn't even give it a second thought. Literally Kevin's phone rang as he handed the stranger all of his money. Kevin answered his phone and it was his cousin who called to ask Kevin if he could come right over to help him fix his car for $100. He was up $80 in an instant of his selfless giving to a stranger. Kevin's generosity had everything to do with him seeing a fellow man in need with an open heart. Kevin had no doubt life would support him. And it did without delay.....he was in perfect flow in his intention and tapped into what he was inspired to do.

Be the energy of your dream

Did you ever think about acting how your future self would act? Tapping into the energy of who you aspire to be. Say you wish to be promoted to a Vice President of a company as a goal. How would your ideal vision Vice President of a company act? How would she/he think and feel? What qualities does your ideal leader possess and how does she/he make others feel inspired and appreciated? How does he/she dress? What kind of language does he/she use? Motivate yourself and inspire yourself to do your present job with that enthusiasm and embody those qualities and the same energy of a strong, positive leader.

You may start to act as the Vice President would act. Such as interacting with outstanding character, be engaging in conversations, be a really attentive listener, be centered and in control of your emotions, be confident in your efforts and notice and others good qualities and efforts. Be in integrity with your words and actions, remember to compliment people for things well done. Share the love and excellence NOW.

Remember the beginning of me embodying the qualities of a homecoming queen to overcome my shyness and outcome of what actually happened without expectation? Act as if you already are what you desire. It really can show up!

- I was watching ESPN and saw that Serena Williams father said to her around 11 years old as she was hitting the tennis ball, *hit the ball like you are at Wimbledon.* Inspire others and speak greatness over them.

- I heard that Ellen Degeneres used to say she was going to be the first woman comedian on the Tonight Show to be invited to sit on Johnny Carson's couch. She was! Speak it and believe it my friends.

- Jim Carrey used to go to the top of Mulholland Drive and visualize and really feel and embody being a fulfilled and successful actor. Even writing out a check to himself for $10,000,000 for acting services rendered. His dreams unfolded as he envisioned.

Empower your words, your vision, acting as if you already are living it…..…. yes….do that!

Time to let it go ~

If you have done your part to the best of your ability and there's nothing left to do, well then let go…..it's time to simply get back to you. Give it up your tight grip and just get on with your day. R E L A X and ask the Universe take over.

It's not giving up by letting go. Absolutely do your part to the best of your abilities, but surrender the rest. When we feel we can't do anymore and life seems to fight us when we insist on our way and something is not working, recognize the **energy of resistance.** Like the Universe is saying, hey this isn't right timing, or nope not here, or maybe your focus could be better served elsewhere. It's like rebooting your computer by shifting your attention for a bit. Reboot and refresh!

I have learned though many experiences, forcing my way isn't the way to go. I even declare it out loud when I see clearly I am hitting a brick wall to the best of my efforts. "Ok Universe, I see you don't what me to do this right now, so it's yours." "I'm going to go play, thank you!" I have had the best miracles where things solve themselves or the most unbelievable answers are delivered as if magic delivery service into my lap when I turned my attention elsewhere!

It is said, *Stand Ye Still and rest on the Lord, and not on your own understanding.* We don't need to know what's happening always. But we can recognize the language in the energy presenting itself. Recognizing when you are in flow or when you are not in flow. When you recognize the energy of resistance - just let go. Returning focus back into your heart center and body in the present moment. Go play or go do anything else. You will be back in flow and allowing the best answers to come to you in ease and grace.

BEING THE MOST POWERFUL YOU! ~

The road to being the most powerful and the happiest version of yourself is being true to yourself in your authenticity and in self love. When you are clear in the areas of knowing your undeniable value and how you truly feel at a core level in what matters to you in life, things become much better.

You communicate better because you are clear in who you are and what you feel. You are stronger in the sense of only allowing or accepting what YOU choose to allow. You get to a point where you can not stomach to betray yourself ever again. And the biggest component in aligning with your true self is to also remembering to be in alignment with God. We are one.

It is so helpful to learn what the Universe's communication feels like to you, what is your personal language and relationship with God? To speak to the Divine, to trust you have put something in motion whether it is a question or prayer, and to understand the feedback you are receiving. This combo of self love, awareness and your God relationship is a recipe that sets you up for the best and highest path.

The following practices enhance your journey because you are clear in who you are and your needs and what you are putting out energetically. You naturally draw in your best because you filter what is being presented from a fulfilled empowered place.

1. LOVE YOURSELF AUTHENTICALLY AND WITH DEDICATION

Number one to enhancing your life and your energy is loving yourself with a fierce dedication. Who you are at your deepest level is for you to discover! To walk always through life in SELF LOVE and your desired intention of how you wish to be in the world. God made you just the way you are *on purpose*. Others may try to influence or critique us based off of *their* expectations and desires.

Be clear in your sense of self and in your self-respect. Knowing yourself at a core level is valuable because you are clearer around what you will accept and what you will not accept. Clarity and communication breeds greater happiness in the long run. You being your best advocate.

Loving yourself enough to communicate your needs sets you up for more fulfillment and less disappointment. Allowing and recognizing your emotions, and staying in tune authentically to yourself is really a gift for not only you but everyone in your life.

Things become easier in your interactions because people know the respect you have for yourself. There is no one who can take advantage and also there are less misunderstandings because you communicate more clearly if something isn't for you. Of course there will be those who protest, but that is for them to deal with now isn't it? Don't let people sway you from having a voice in being your own best advocate. *You never have to apologize for your needs or what you feel.*

Also a big thing to remember is not to wait for someone else to fulfill you. YOU take actions steps to fulfill your needs. You step in for yourself when you need something. **Ask yourself, *what can I do to love myself more today?*** What would fill me right now? Pencil something you love into your schedule! Many times we are so focused on our to do list and caring for others we forget to take time for ourselves. It's time for you my friend to include yourself in the people that you love!

> *Tend to your body, your mind, emotions and spirit with love and care. Avoid self-judgment or self-criticism. Only great love and make this a regular practice!*

Golden sisterly advice

My sister Patti once gave to me the best advise when I was a young mom as she saw me being overwhelmed at times. I had the busyness of being a mom to small children while being business owner. I was trying to run everything perfectly and keeping everyone happy. Which balancing too much seems to be a way of life for so many of us doesn't it? Like we win a prize for being the most exhausted.

Patti's said to me on one day, *"Remember to take the time to take care of yourself." "No one else will do it for you or give you permission."*

I used to think doing things for myself was selfish. And I mistook busyness as success. I would think I'll get to me eventually.....well that never happened. There is a vast difference between self-care and being selfish. It is essential to nurture that part of you to feel fulfilled as a person. And truly you have more to give when you feel happy.

Take action for yourself when you need something you crave in your spirit. EVERYONE will benefit! It could be a massage, or reading a book, some time with your friends, or maybe go surfing or for a run. Refresh your system with care and love yourself. Self-care may at times may be standing up for yourself, or asking for help....and speaking your truth which let me tell you *is* being spiritual.

At the beginning of me choosing to walk this path I interpreted being a spiritual person as being kind and selfless. As Nancy said to me over 20 years ago, being spiritual does not mean being a doormat for others.

To me now *spirituality is living consciously with our God connection and our connection to self, living with awareness and authenticity not only with SELF but to be in awareness of how we can be of service to our brothers and sisters in our community, on our planet. Authentically caring for who you are, dedicated to your purpose, your spirit and your body is honoring God by taking care of the gift to the world he made that is YOU.*

Manage your energy by starting with loving yourself with great passion, compassion, conviction and care. This is where all the goodness and magic begins. You begin to become fulfilled from within. Life will begin to reflect back love to you.

2. BE CLEAR IN YOUR COMMUNICATION
and setting boundaries

So here we are trying to be in self love, God connection, being in awareness, positive and good in the world. Then someone comes into our bliss and throws our happy vibe. Now what? Well as a practice it serves us to remember who we are and how we wish to be in the world. (The step above.)

This spiritual business isn't all rainbows and unicorns. Eventually we have to deal with challenging or upsetting situations.

Authenticity and integrity to self is where it all begins in opening the door to being truly happy. Before you can be authentically happy in relationships whether personal or with work you must first value yourself. Remember the idea that the Universe holds up a mirror? All relationships will reflect how we feel about ourselves - work and personal.

Have you ever heard the saying you teach people how to treat you? If you accept poor statements or behavior why would someone ever stop? Be clear and have a conversation in what you will accept and in what you expect or would like to see. This will set you up for much better in your experiences professional, romantic, friends and family. Communicate clearly and set boundaries when necessary to honor yourself always.

My experience is if someone is saying something that isn't sitting well with you, or you pushed it aside because you didn't want to address it, it will come up again somehow. Suppressing or ignoring what needs to be addressed will eventually come out sideways if you keep ignoring it. Meaning if you hold something inside of you, the littlest thing done by the other person or even someone else in a similar situation you may overreact because it needs to come up and out energetically. Find the courage to address your feelings brings clarity for all and brings peace and harmony much faster. And then it's done. Energy cleared! Move onto joy.

It also helps communication to not assume the meaning of someone's intention and to get clarity around a person's statement if it is not abundantly clear and it's eating at you. Many times we assume and fill in the blanks and find out we were terribly wrong in our assumption. If you are correct well this provides us an opportunity to communicate what needs to be addressed.

Communicating authentically and staying in your integrity to self and integrity in your respect for others as well, brings peace for everyone involved. Once you take a step towards better communication and honoring your peace, communicating what is important to your happiness, and make this a regular practice, you will find you can't go backwards.

3. DO YOU WANT TO BE RIGHT OR DO YOU WANT TO BE HAPPY?

Here is another side of the coin. Just dropping it. I loved Wayne Dyer's advise when I heard him speak in Philadelphia years ago…..Do you want to be right, or do you want to be happy? More often than not I decide I want peace and happiness. How many times have you been challenged and you know by experience when someone is just giving you a hard time for their own kicks and giggles, or possibly it is more deep rooted for them.

Just dropping your need to prove your point from an ego space and instead choosing an act of love and kindness to yourself and the other person. You can just say ok, wow you are right. It's not like God is taking a tally upstairs. Oh yes, Donna 342 people 215. Lol. People are only coming from their own life experiences and perspectives. Same as you wish to be heard and loved, so do they.

Ask yourself is this really going to matter in 5 years? If no, then just get on with your day. Think of the positive energy you just made room for by choosing to align with peace for yourself and for the other person. Is it worth your energy to be right? What energy do you wish to hold? How do you want to spend your day? Peace and love, or allowing your energy and vibration to be zapped. Sometimes just choosing love and getting on with your day is a great answer!

Michelle Obama to me is an amazing role model of poise, strength, and intelligence. She displayed the best example of this idea of rising above – making her powerful declaration for the world to hear! "**When they go low, we go high!**" Choose love! Let it go!

4. CHOOSE YOUR FOCUS (setting your energy for the day)

Just think how things may go in your day if YOU choose how you wish to be in the world and the energy you set in motion sending it out or your day? Instead of allowing the day to happen TO YOU, you set things in motion with your *conscious self.* Meaning from a higher awareness you can choose what you want to invite into your today. Even before your feet hit the floor.

Tap into the expansive energy of Love and begin to think about what do you wish to experience in your day? It could be as simple as, Let's make it a great day today, or praying for a blessing for yourself and your loves, the world etc. Invite in qualities such as; appreciation, laughter, praise or recognition, joy, success, cooperation, organization, flow, positive, dynamic, prosperity, the happiest or the highest love energy to your day.

> *Taking the time to be aligned ~ set your intention and invite the energy you desire into your day.*

Then check within throughout your day. If things seem off at any point and you feel off track (which happens), you can reset your energy. Again, it's like hitting the refresh button on your computer. Simply bring the thoughts and focus back to the energy of your intention from early.

Let go of the idea of life happening outside of you and to you. ***Energy comes from the inside and travels outward from you.*** *Focus back inside of your own body, your own heart, mind and spirit, as this is your point of creation.*

It's when we allow those moments where the energy outside of us to affect us and throw us off center. Sometimes we allow circumstances to take over our day. Step back, take a minute for a breath and just realign within.

Be patient with yourself, no self judgement if you slipped into old habits. We all get sidetracked. It's always worth the effort to get centered again with your intention and oneness with God/Universe! You can keep a bad day from unfolding and taking on more momentum. Just choose to realign.

REMEMBER.....*THE UNIVERSE IS RESPONDING TO YOU.*

5. KEEP IT POSITIVE

Sometimes when we are alone our minds tend to wander down some familiar habits looking for what's wrong or what is upsetting us in the moment. Or we could obsess with a tight grip trying to be in control of things we don't have control over. Instead of letting your mind flow uncontrollably in habitual patterns, simply and lovingly say when the ranting mind starts….it's ok I see what's happening, this is just a habit. (Be easy on yourself just be proud you are catching it.)

Really just stop for just a minute. Invite and breathe in the energy of ease and grace, peace and love. The key is how you FEEL.

The idea here is to simply practice feeling good. Whatever the topic is not as important as is the energy of feeling better in your vibe. What do you love? Is it how you feel while at the beach that is your bliss, or out in nature hiking by a waterfall, what was one of the best times of your life that you can connect with that AWESOME feeling. Was it the birth of your child, winning a championship that your loved? Feel into that greatness that WOOO HOOO feeling. Connect to that feeling and energy for a while.

Or envision trying on what you would love to do on your bucket list and see yourself doing it in your vision. Try it for a bit and see how you feel in your body, in your heart. Hopefully you can feel these wonderful moments and are now emanating happy heart expansive energy? Think of this practice as time well spent. Investing attention on how you're feeling, and what you maybe creating from this space. Your future happy is unfolding with this great mojo you have going. Remember....Mirror Mirror!

6. HABITS OF GRATITUDE

I know this is not a new concept I am bringing up. But gratitude is so powerful and has great value energetically. It can have a beautiful effect in your body and it puts you in a higher vibrational state. If you haven't ever tried it maybe start a gratitude journal, find a little notebook you can carry with you. Make a list of at least 3 things either in the morning, or before bed of what you are grateful for in your life. Or verbally say them outloud, thank you God for.....(you fill in the blank.)

Have you heard of the idea of a gratitude jar? I love this idea. Where you drop in slips of paper with notes written of experiences from your day you were grateful for, or person you are grateful for, things about yourself that you are grateful for. Yes, include yourself in the list of people you are grateful for. Your healthy legs, your award winning smile, you may be proud of a kindness you extended today. When you feel off or down you can go back to that jar and pull out some slips of paper to reconnect into that feeling of gratitude in those moments!

Try spending a minute before bed thinking back upon your day taking note of the good moments. Sit just for a few moments with appreciation for those experiences. Recalling at days end....yep, that was pretty awesome.... oh I forgot about that happened....that was really cool.

Do you see if you think about things that are good feeling to end your day instead of thinking about your worries? You are broadcasting out beautiful vibrations to the universe as you drift off to sleep. Your mind becomes more peaceful, your body as will let go a and transition better and more restful sleep.

To me it's like making that little deposit into your bank account. It keeps growing with amazing dividends for you!

If it's bedtime and you seem to not to be able to turn off your mind of worry, or your to do list…..keep a notebook by your bed that you can jot your thoughts that are keeping you from peace. See it like transferring it out of your mind and body through your arm and out of your hand releasing your concerns onto the paper. You won't forget to take care of these things as you will see your to do list in the morning. This trick is very helpful to stop your mind from the vicious loop at bedtime. Back to peace and gratitude.

7. CLEAR YOUR ENERGY ~ What could the energy showing up be telling you?

What if we seem to keep having experiencing similar experiences that we wish would stop? Does it seem as though there are times you keep repeating circumstances over and over like in the movie Groundhog's Day? The same things happening with different people, at different jobs, different friendships, different relationships, etc? Maybe it's your wake up call to pay attention and to do some deep diving as to what has been showing up for you. What do you need to see with in these experiences?

The concept that life is a mirror was a hard pill for me to swallow when it was introduced to me years ago. The idea that we are responsible for what is showing up in our lives because of the energy we hold? The idea that life is reflecting back to us how are on the inside. Can you imagine how Sherry may have felt hearing that bit of information having lived in an abusive relationship? How absurd! She didn't ask to be abused!

Sherry thought back to her upbringing and wondered if she could see any similarities in how she felt at any point of her life that reminded her of her experiences in her partnership. Much of Sherry's day as a child was about being on her best behavior because that was expected. At times she was a little fearful about repercussions of her actions. Most of the time she would get into trouble not even really understanding what she did wrong. Now mind you she had beautiful loving moments, but this is what we do. Our interpretation of the information that impacts us can be held in our energy.

The good news is we are the grownups now and can have a new, more mature awareness, perspective and understanding. When we see that old energy surfacing in our experiences in the now *it can be recognized and cleared. And the grown up you can choose better and make more empowering choices!*

It took Sherry a bit, she saw it. By observing the similarities in her experiences she was empowered to clear it. There was an energy thread that kept being recreated throughout Sherry's life for her until finally she decided to say ENOUGH. NO MORE. The energy she held onto since childhood matched her up with another opportunity in her adulthood to experience this energy again. It keeps getting bigger and bigger until you can't go down a path one more time without making some changes.

Sherry created greater happiness for herself by taking the time to unpack and sit in the feelings around an energy she recognized. And moving forward she has graduated to higher self-worth and self-respect and found a relationship that reflects the respect she has for herself.

When something triggers you, it's simply the Universe is showing you something that would benefit you to clear or heal. Is there something that you don't enjoy showing up in your experiences? What does it remind you in regards to the feelings around it? Where did you ever feel that similarly in the past? Is there a common denominator? Chances are you may see something from a few years back, but take it further. Most experiences come all the way back from childhood, and have been occurring in a theme or pattern.

I strongly believe in finding a good therapist or counselor or coach to create wellness and learning to process in healthy ways. Supporting yourself with a good energy healer whether it be reiki, healing touch, tapping, acupuncture or Jin Shin. Maybe yoga or running is your meditation or medicine. So many ways to help release and clear for your good and wellness, mentally, emotionally, and spiritually. Your happiness and peace is worth the work involved to reach freedom and joy in your spirit.

Energy that's not cleared is repeated in your experiences.

Releasing and *forgiving* people and circumstances is clearing it for YOUR good! I remember when Carol my Reiki Teacher told me that people are doing their best they can for their level of awareness at the time. What if someone IS actually doing their best? That thought alone is very freeing to me.

8. CHANGING YOUR WORDS TO CREATE WHAT YOU DESIRE!

Just think about what you repeatedly are saying out loud, talking to your family, friends coworkers, anyone who will listen. Try thinking of your "word as your wand," as Florence Scovel Shinn titled a chapter in the book The Game of Life and How to Play it. There is a creative resonance in our words.

So what if you catch yourself complaining out of habit. Or saying something critical about yourself or someone else. All it takes once you recognize your thoughts and words you speak that have been that is not leaving you feeling great, just say to yourself, ok STOP! Let me just redirect what I am saying to better. I am going to speak positivity over my life.

When you finally have some time alone take a minute to speak out loud your desires or declare statements as if they are already true. Something like, "Life is unfolding in the most enjoyable ways for me" "I am letting go and enjoying my day!" "Wonderful changes are happening." "I am loving the beauty unfolding in life." I am in alignment with greater prosperity and life is getting easier." Or whatever evokes a positive feeling for you. Speak it out loud! "I am aligned with fantastic success, I have the Midas touch." "I am talented and my efforts are always recognized and appreciated." "I have such fulfilling relationships, I am so happy." "I only attract the best, and all my good is unfolding." Some statements will feel great, some may not. Speak things that light your own inner fire of enthusiasm!

Be mindful of what you are saying....try it for a week with dedication. If you start to say something negative it's ok, just jump back on to the love energy train and try again. Be easy with yourself, and love your future self enough to pay attention to what you are saying from this point forward.

8. STAY INSPIRED ~ Find books or videos of inspiration

Another great way to manage your energy is to read empowering books or videos keep you inspired and learning. Try getting up just a few minutes early each day for some "you" time. Start dedicating your morning to positivity to get on the right footing and energy. Even if you set aside 10 minutes for reading something inspiring or even listen in your car on the way to work.

Whether it's a Daily Devotional that resonates with you, I love one titled, Jesus Calling. Speaking so much of that oneness and focus on God and handing concerns over. Tony Robbins is a great motivator and helps empower you, or Joel Osteen speaks in the most inspiring ways and biblical promises. I actually renewed my sirius radio just to hear Joel! Mike Dooley is a delightfully inspirational man, fabulous author and speaker about how the Universe works in an easy to understand way. I loved Manifesting Change, and Infinite Possibilities. So much that I got certified as an Infinite Possibilities Trainer.

Every morning I would also often grab books or listen to wisdom by Wayne Dyer, Louise Hay, Deepak Chopra, Sonya Choquette, Esther and Jerry Hicks, Colette Baron Reid, Gabby Bernstein, Marianne Williamson as a few of my favs.

The most empowering books for me was recommended by my friend Deb at work years ago that I mentioned above. I love that it ties spiritual principles with bible foundations. This book is titled, "Game of Life and How to Play It." It was written by Florence Scovel Shinn who is an author from the 1920's! Wonderfully powerful statements and affirmations in this book, and wonderful wisdom.

9. BE AWARE OF SOCIAL MEDIA or
how you spend your free time

I feel this is worth mentioning. I see so many people who get consumed by social media. It's the first thing so many people do as a go to much of their day. It's fantastic to connect and actually find inspiration. Just saying to be mindful when on social media of the feelings you are having and where it leads your thoughts.

We are flooded with so much information, opinions, visuals that may not leave us feeling so good or may not influence us in positive ways. Sometimes we compare ourselves with the story or image people post. We may go into self judgement of not feeling good enough or maybe a bit of anger being annoyed at someone's views they are putting out there. It can keep you from living in the now, being with your kids, your spouse. Life is for living!

Spend time doing things that fill you and are fun, that leave you joyful, loved and peaceful. Bring what feeds your vibe throughout your day. Love you on every level and the life you are creating!

CHAPTER 15

Mood and Energy Enhancers

Yes bring it! Let's connect to higher vibes. Sometimes we need to be professional, focus for work or need to study and not be distracted by something bothering us. Sometimes we need a break from our bad mood and as much as we try we just can't shake it. We may want to fully enjoy and make the best our time with our family, our friends or our partner. Sometimes we don't know how to put something aside so we can enjoy ourselves.

Why would we allow something that happened earlier rock our world with our special time with the people who really matter the most. Instead of allowing the petty cares or frustrations to grow and take momentum, we can stop the motion completely by refocusing. If it's important know you will readdress something later. For now allowing high vibe flow to this moment you wish to enjoy!

Here are a few ideas to help you connect to your spirit and center when you want to feel better quickly.

TOOLS TO HELP YOU SHIFT YOUR MOOD AND RAISE YOUR VIBE

1.Music

The number one quickest and most obvious shift for so many of us is music. Music has transformative powers. It speaks to our soul and evokes different emotions in us. Keep some power songs on your playlist. What I choose depends on my mood. If I am not myself or low energy I will play fun songs. Or if I need calming like when I work from home and I am pretty intense because all I am trying to accomplish so much, I may put on something more soothing like meditation or classical music.

This past summer I had some goings on that had me rattled me and I wanted to sit and deal with it to clear the energy. The natural thing for people to do is to try to help you be happy and fix you, lol. I love spending time with my girl and her friends. I couldn't help myself but give in to the moment when Jadin conspired with her friend Hannah to shift my mood. They whispered between the passenger seat of my car and the back seat. My daughter grabbed my phone, connected to bluetooth and put on Kanye West and Jamie Foxx's Gold Digger and blasted it. Jadin, Hannah and I always go nuts when that song comes on my car stereo. I looked at them like nice try but it's not going to work right now. Well that lasted for about 30 seconds. Full on car dancing for all of us. What's your song that always shifts you?

2. MINDFULNESS ~Getting present

This practice is great if your mind seems to have taken a ride on a runaway train. When as much as you try, you can't seem to control where your mind is going. So what does getting present mean really? It means to not dwell on the past, or worry about the future, just BE in the now. Getting out of your head. If you know you are a co-creator why would we want to think around things that makes you feel badly on a consistent basis?

When you are being mindful you are not worrying about the future, or obsessing on the past or what this person did to you or a situation weighing on your mind. Instead your mind is occupied simply with the observing and being fully present with right now. In the following exercise by shifting and directing your focus and observation to what is happening each moment you can stop the runaway train and find peace. Most of the time anyway, the right now is really ok. Give this present moment your all.

STOP THE PANIC AND GAIN CONTROL OF THE MIND

Let's see what being present and mindful could look like. Look around the room where you are right a now. Keep breathing mindful breaths, deeply and slowly as you practice this exercise. What do you *see*? (name say 10 things your eye is drawn to) What do you *hear*? (name 5 things, outside, inside, your breathing, even the sound of you swallowing.) How is the temperature to you, what do you *feel* in your body and how does it feel in your body, tension, tightness? Feel the hardness of the chair under your legs, touch the fabric and texture with your skin.

Practice observing ~ WHAT'S HAPPENING IN YOUR BODY?

Let me give you an example as I am right in this moment what this can look like. I am noticing as I type my fingers are a bit swollen. (I ate for my soul, not my health the last 24 hours.....lol) Taking a deep breath..... feel the air travel through your nose, down to your lungs. Slow down your breathing, really focusing deeply on your breath and feeling your chest expanding as your lungs fill, to where you notice the muscles in your back expanding as well, feel it stretch. Feel your belly rise and fall with each breath. Where do you feel restricted or tight in your body? Relax your muscles starting from the top of your head section by section down to your feet.

WHAT DO YOU HEAR? WHAT DO YOU NOTICE?

I am hearing a train whistle blow in the distance right now. I notice how I feel love in my heart when I hear that train. I notice of that feeling of love produced peace with in me. Also it is so quiet that I can hear the hum of the refrigerator. I heard a crack and looked up to see my candle flickering on my bookshelf and I watch it for a minute. I feel a cozy homey feeling watching the dancing golden flame flicker before me.

All of this attention to your surroundings through your different senses do you see you are not worrying? The presence is your focus. All of sudden you notice the tension in your body is lessoned and you feel a bit calmer. Because in most circumstances, you are truly ok right in this moment. Suddenly you are not dwelling on what upsets you. Recognizing in this moment.....all is ok. Your turn, give this a try. Next time you get a little stressed just give this a whirl. It's really a quick solution to shift to being more relaxed.

3. <u>Create the time and space for</u> <u>MANAGING YOUR ENERGY</u>

I know those of you with crazy surroundings and schedules are thinking you don't get a moments peace. A demanding workload, endless home responsibilities, soccer practice, noisy kids, or a moody spouse or coworker. Remember I have all of that too and understand the frustration you could feel trying to find a minute to even simply hear your own thoughts. You feel you can't literally breathe sometimes.

Well that is exactly what you need to do. B R E A T H E. In those stressful moments we find ourselves holding our breath. Recognize if you are holding your breath, unclench your hands, let go of where you are holding tension in your body and just breathe. Right where you are. Or find anywhere else to be for a minute. Make any excuse to grab some peace. Even if people don't understand, don't tell them, just do it. I used to just go into the bathroom at work when I saw I needed to regroup and refresh my vibe.

Breathe, stretch your arms over head bend in half to the floor, come back up and stretch some more. Take a second to focus within your body and soul, recalibrate, pray and ask for help in getting calm. I am peaceful. I am peace. B R E A T H E again. Feel your muscles relax. Shake it out. Finding 30 seconds or 5 minutes of peace really can be enough of a renewal to juice up your vibe and to feel better.

Get out for a walk outside where the focus is on feeling peace into your body, breathing the fresh air, and the movement with intention to let go of releasing. Getting peaceful and centered with in maybe repeating a mantra. You will be surprised how you can shift quickly and clear your head and feel refreshed by shifting gears for a few minutes.

If you forget to check in, maybe set your alarm and take 2 minutes a few times a day. Refresh yourself in good energy!

4. Meditate

Meditation can take many forms – walking, sitting, running, gardening, baking, or even doing the dishes can be a form of meditation. For me going into my heart space and getting creative while doing hair color is a form of oneness and meditation. The key is to connect to the oneness by going with in, feeling into your heart space and being in alignment. Getting quiet in your mind, relaxing your body, breathing, being fully present with your task or whatever it is you are doing. We care for our body with proper nutrition, we study to grow our minds. I say it again… we are body, mind AND spirit.

Take the time to see what your spirit has to say. By connecting quieting your mind you connect to hear your higher and authentic self, while listening and feeling into God's presence and wisdom. After meditation my day flows better, I hear messages and guidance better. I feel happier and handle life's little surprises with much more grace.

If your mind tends to wander or you find it difficult, try a guided meditation. Carol my reiki teacher preferred a walking meditation daily in the woods to connect as opposed to sitting and going with in. What will work for you to find that space and listen to your higher self and the Divine inspiration? Try a few ideas on for size. Do what works best for YOU.

Youtube has unlimited guided meditations or look up on Hayhouse.com in their online store for fantastic books on or audio meditations. Amazon you can download meditations right to your phone. Deepak Chopra and

Oprah Winfrey wonderful quarterly meditations around a certain topic you can do for free at a time convenient for you.

5. Focus on LOVE!

YEP, I know this sounds a bit airy fairy if you are new to this. Truly focus on what brings you that love feeling. What in your life makes your heart burst and feel warm and fuzzy, or a whole body YES. Connect to that thought of what produces a feeling of that whole body encompassing joy. Keep that love feeling going for a few minutes. Is it a person, or a place or event that you recall? Can you feel a shift to "yes that feels amazing," when you recall something you absolutely love? Whatever it is really FEEL into it and HOLD that feeling in your body. THEN...expand it beyond and around your body by a couple of feet expanding outward.

Once you get there, turn up the volume. Just like you turn up the dial like before we had remotes. See yourself take a hold of that dial and turn it way up, the vibration of love in its intensity of the feeling, feel the energy getting stronger and bigger. Hold it there that feeling of expanding love energy. Feel yourself bathing in this beautiful love.

6. Send out blessings

I came across a great self-paced class years ago that I absolutely love from Mindvalley Academy. This class was all about energy, which really resonated with my beliefs and experiences in being a Reiki Master. I already was living my life being conscious of energy.

There were a new few ideas new to me in the class with Christie Marie Sheldon that I use often today. Her class was called Love and Above, and I highly recommend this course through Mindvalley. The curriculum talked about when we when we are in the in a state of joy, love, blessings, gratitude which all measure over the vibration of 500 or above we attract better for our lives and manifest with ease. The better the state of our thoughts and feelings the higher the vibration, the easier it is to attract what you desire.

I have told so many people about Christie, I adore her. One of the things I learned through the course was even blessing people through my day not only sends good to them, but it raises our vibration as well. Win, win! But you can start with you.

"I bless myself with pure love and light, I bless myself with purest source energy."

You can send out blessings to a situation, to a person, to your children. Even a building, or a stranger in a car, or a mailbox, a tree, a baby, or a dog. Keep sending out blessings, it not only raises your vibration and puts you in a more connected peaceful state and awareness. I realized by sending blessings your mind is occupied on good high vibe practices. Our minds are busy with great things, and free from worry or fears, or complaining!

Try also sending God's energy ahead to your day. When I started teaching new classes for multiple manufacturers I was very nervous. I was concerned how I would remember all of the facts and technical information of all of these brands. Plus I had heard horror stories how people treated the teacher.

I invited in God into my day. I envisioned a white light coming down into myself, then I would send the energy ahead of me to my day and everyone I will encounter. I invited God's light to into my classes and all who attended. I asked that I am a blessing them they are a blessing to me. We are blessed by being together.

Try sending blessings to people to your day, even to inanimate objects, trees, babies, cars whatever you feel drawn to bless. Observe how your day goes from the ordinary to extraordinary!

7. <u>The Pendulum Swing</u>

This gem I credit Louise Laffey my beautiful and wise Wish™ and New Heart Movement Teacher. It is a super quick and simple yet powerful tool to shift us to more relaxed. I find when I feel overwhelmed it is very comforting.

Let me explain how this works. I would like for you to think of a crying baby. All out of sorts, screaming really upset. What is a common remedy to we do to help calm and soothe them? **We rock them**! We may rock front to back, we may sway from side to side. We set the tone by shushing them. Shhhhhhhhh. Calmly and softly….. Shhhhhhhhh. The rocking motion can be very soothing. But it resets the energy, and don't we try to BE the calm and try to relax our body to have the babies calm as well? Relax for yourself and begin the motion.

Your Turn ~The Seated Pendulum Swing

Get comfortable in your seat, but sit up straight. Rest your hands on your lap or to your side. Start with a deep breath in, let the tension drop from your body, relax your muscles. Be present with your breath and start rocking side to side, left to right, left to right. Keeping your butt stationary but swinging your upper body left to right and keep repeating the motion. Left, right, left, right, keeping your spine in alignment but relaxed, moving it like a pendulum hanging from a clock with the slow motion. As you make a wide enough swing to make like a "V" with your butt the center bottom or the "V". Moving your upper body to the left to then to the right, left to right, left to right. Like tick, tock, back and forth. Cleansing deep breaths as you go.

When you start the swing, you begin with greater motion in a stronger back and forth for a bit until you start to feel calmer. Then reduce the swing less and less wide, bringing it to a smaller back and forth motion bringing the V to a smaller left and right motion, slowing it down until you feel yourself naturally stop. Keep breathing. How does that feel? Check to see if you need to do it again. You can also try this standing.

Notice how you can feel the energy where you were holding your tension. Does it feel a bit more relaxed? What is happening is your heart is taken of it's axis of the panic energetically and recalibrating. Rebooting your system. You can reset and refresh in literally a minute.

8. <u>Get out of Dodge!</u>

Change the scenery. Sometimes when we are in the same space, we keep repeating the same thoughts in our minds over and over. There are no distractions. So leave from the environment where you are and go anywhere else.

Get out among people and shift your focus.....say hello.....window shop. The idea is to get out of your own head, out of your own way and the vicious loop of what you can't seem to let go of in your mind. It can help when you change your physical environment and the shift the scenery. Even if you are in a terrible mood, eventually you may have talk or respond to somebody when out in public, or notice something pleasing. Ask yourself where would I really like to go right now?

Nurture yourself to a cup of tea or a latte and sit in a cafe, go to Barnes and Noble to find inspiration, get outside in nature, whatever it is you feel guided or inspired to do. Target is one place that shifts me quickly, lol. It's so much fun! Be kind to yourself while you are out and let your self talk be as you would your best friend. Love yourself in this moment in ways you seek fulfillment right now.

9. <u>Ho'oponono</u>

This tool I have found to be ultra-transformative. My friend Tara told my friends and I how her mom introduced her to this book. It called, *The Easiest Way to Live, by Mabel Katz.* All of us in my little vibe tribe really enjoyed this book and saw some powerful shifts in how we felt and what was showing up in our world. I recently was just telling someone who was feeling anxious around something to say these phrases with me and notice if he felt it in his body. His eyes opened wide and said oh my God I can feel it. It feels really good.

Ho'oponopono is all about the Ancient Hawaiian art of forgiveness. It is said that saying these phrases, which ever one appeals to you, a combination of the phrases, or all of them, resets us to clear what we are holding onto from a memory. Even what we don't recognize what we are holding onto. The practice helps us restore to our original purity of heart, align with the Divine, clean the memory and heal. You don't have to understand it to experience lighter and better feelings and the effects of the practice.

I LOVE YOU. I AM SORRY. PLEASE FORGIVE ME. THANK YOU.

The idea is that as I have already spoken about that WE are recreating from our memories we are holding onto in our subconscious and I add here energetically. We attract everything in our life. And we are 100% responsible for what we create. I have read a few books on the topic and have put into practice Ho'oponopono. I absolutely see outcomes shift and feel the energetic shift. The great thing is you don't have to fully understand to see the effects in calming you, aligning you, surrendering to the Divine, and bringing more light into your situation. It is an act of healing you, and situations. I find this practice can shift people quickly when I take them through the process.

And again this is the abbreviated clip, I encourage you to read more around this topic. I find Mabel Katz easy to understand and I resonate with her messages on Ho'oponono.

Try this when there is something that is stealing your peace or a problem. Remember we created this experience, it's not outside of you. Go with in. Below are a few steps to see what appeals to you if you would like to give it a try.

- **Say, "Whatever it is within me that created this condition, I love you, I'm sorry, please forgive me, thank you."** Whatever it is you are going through, know that you are inviting in the Divine to this circumstance and memory to be released, surrendering, healing, and cleaning the memory within you of what created this situation that is upsetting you. (Keep repeating while feeling with in your body and breathing.) See how you feel. Say this over and over until you feel a shift.

- **Hold a vision of someone or a situation that seems to upset or concern you.** As you picture the person in your mind in front of you or a situation .....say, I'm sorry, I forgive you, I love you, thank you. Or just any of the phrases over and over or a combination. You will know intuitively what you need.

There maybe someone who needs to be forgiven or a situation that you have had problems letting go. Or even wish to send the highest and best outcome to something. Whatever it is, I like to invite God and his wisdom into the process. You free yourself energetically by cleaning the memory and healing. I myself have taken it further and used the phrases to send energy to something like a circumstance unfolding. It always produces the highest blessings in the unfolding for me. Try it. I absolutely love this practice!

Everyone when asked to try this, literally within a minute say to me I feel better! It's a powerful practice and can help you shift to feeling better and smoother and miraculous changes in your life when you really work with this Ancient Art of Forgiveness. Give it a whirl my friends. It's an amazing tool!

10. <u>Laughter</u>

Being light and joyful is so good for your soul and vibration! When you feel off sometimes we just need to lighten up. Not to take life so seriously. Tap into whatever helps you feel that open hearted laughing. Who is your tribe of people who are fun or a person who just has that fun hearted vibe you can call or ask to get together. I am a huge fan of comedy, I listen to Sirius comedy channels while driving, go to comedy clubs, I love watching old sitcoms or funny movies, laughing with my family and friends. Smiling produces a positive response within our body and energy. Love, laugh, and go enjoy your funny! Life can be heavy if we dwell on what's heavy. Or we can shift it for a while, and shift our mood!

You are so powerful!

The great news is whatever is showing up is your world you created, you are that powerful. *If you can create what showed up until now, just imagine how you can create knowing how to manage your energy!*

CHAPTER 16

Signs and Guidance

I couldn't end this book without giving you some ideas what signs and communication from the Universe could look like if you aren't already aware. This is where life gets to be so fun for me. Seeing signs in your world that you just know have meaning, like a signpost along the way to let you know, YES....keep up the good work.....you are not alone. Many ways for the invisible to make themselves known to you.

Are you ready to dip your toe in the pool of having the two way street with God? Life will become more inspiring, fulfilling, joyful, magical and miraculous when you ask to be guided, or even just asking for signs to give you reassurance that they hear you and are helping. Pay attention, very soon you will actually receive answers you are recognizing! As I mentioned a few times, I find you will receive messages in a language that has significance for YOU.

It seems to me that many right now who are opening on their path start with seeing numbers that repeat often. I know myself I started being curious by seeing numbers repeat about 20 years ago. It was unmistakable and caught my attention. I am finding people who I happen to become friends with will call me up and ask, I keep seeing for example 555. Or 11:11. Why is this happening? Does it mean something? Oh, yes it does. Spirit is getting your attention and you are noticing. Hurray and congratulations!

Where do you look for signs or guidance?

So a couple of things, the first is to just live your life and be in the present. Meaning if your mind is consumed with focusing on your life or your to do list, or worry.....you are distracted. You could be missing an exciting sign or communication that is meant for you.

Being present is important because the truck passing you on the highway is happening NOW. The song playing on the radio that was special to your mom who passed away is happening NOW. That commercial on TV totally repeated exactly just what you said seconds before is happening in the NOW.

You will feel sometimes like.... well that's crazy that just happened, isn't that a strange coincidence? Nope, it's not. It's called synchronicity! I wonder if that is a sign? You can bet it is! Say thank you, you have just been shown you are in alignment. You are being supported, loved, being cheered on and are in flow!

When you align with the Divine and invite God in you will see things unfold in new ways that feel so exciting. Signs will show up in a ways that stand out to *YOU* as significant. If something strongly catches your attention and jumps out to you don't second guess it, it IS significant! No question!

Just know it is normal to question this process of being aware of messages at first. Especially if you tell someone who is not really into this kind of thing. Someone who even loves you may laugh you are putting value into signs. They may try to convince you it's only a coincidence. If that's the case, just keep your new little treasures to yourself.

Most of my signs for me these days show up on side of trucks, license plates, songs on the radio, synchronicities or numbers jumping out that have significance. Hearing someone mentioning something in conversation that I had just spoken about is also a message. Getting information you needed at the right time showing you are supported! Notice what you are thinking about or saying or praying about when you stumble across a sign. The timing is no accident.

You may find feathers or coins when someone is reaching out or giving you an 'atta boy! (Yes, feathers or coins.) See below for a quick list of ways as a quick reference to keep your eyes open to spiritual help right away! Of course not limited to this list, but something to use a quick reference for a bit till you get the idea if this is new to you.

Signs and ways to recognize Spirit

1. Coins
2. Feathers
3. A song playing that is meaningful to you or to a person who passed, or has a certain significance in some way
4. Flickering lights, or electrical glitches that catch your attention (and the timing of the flicker.)
5. Repeating number sequences or symbols
6. Seeing sparks of light - this is angel energy
7. Seeing orbs or colored lights (Check out your pics or videos for orbs!)
8. Goosebumps or chills (to me this is confirmation of truth of what you are saying or thinking)
9. Sudden temperature change in the room or a certain area in the room
10. Scents that catch your attention (unexplained)
11. Books falling off of the shelf maybe is meant to read or has a specific message for you to checkout. (I find I am drawn to a book like a magnet. Calling me to pick it up and turn to a certain page)
12. Synchronicity always lets you know you are being supported or are in flow.
13. Bells ringing (either church bells in the timing, or seemingly out of nowhere)
14. Doves, cardinals or specific birds and their symbolism
15. Butterflies

16. Dragonflies
17. Hear a positive voice (thought) with a brief message.

Just start by practicing awareness and being open. Ask for a sign to let you know the Universe hears you and is around you. Or ask how would they like to show you when your guardian angel is around? Such as a coin. I know when I first started I looked so hard for signs I was overdoing it. Seeing signs is more about being easy about it and observant.

Oh say can you see? ~

I did not know when I started seeing sparks in the darkness while I feeding Jadin her bottle in the middle of the night what it could be. I sensed it was something mystical but didn't know what. So to be certain it wasn't my health, I went to the eye doctors wondering if there was something wrong with my eyes. I said, "I see sparks that light up through the darkness when I'm feeding the baby." The doctor just looked at me like I lost my mind and he responded, yeah....I've never heard of anything like that.

Within a week after I saw the eye doctor, I read that we may at times see angels as a quick spark of light in our vision, or an angel trail. Which is like seeing a burst of a spark or a light that trail that to me looks like a single firework on the 4th of July.

I often see sparks around people while we are chatting. It lets me know they are being authentic or they are being supported. I mostly see blue sparks around people or white. Blue is Archangel Michael the angel of protection, clearing negativity and life purpose. White is your guardian angel and Green is Archangel Raphael the angel of healing. There are many more colors and angel energy but those are the angels I typically see.

Your own body is the best tool for guidance ~ messages inside of you

Why is your body the best tool? Well it houses your spirit, the all-knowing part of you that is directly connected and a part of God. If you take the time to learn to understand how something feels within your body when you tune into yourself, into your very own vibration you will always have access to your best tool. It available for answers 24/7.

I am sure you can think of many times when you have felt goosebumps all over. Did it seem to come after someone said something or you said something? This is validation that whatever was just said is truth. Even people who are not spiritual will say, oh my God I just got chills when you said that.

How can you develop recognizing yes or no in your body?

One way is for you begin with **asking questions** such as how does this make me feel if I imagine taking THIS action? Notice how you **feel in your body.** Then try asking another question and compare how you felt in your body with the another option in how that felt. I used to practice my accuracy by asking myself a yes no question that I would see an answer to that question soon. Such as will Susie be at the party tonight? Yes or No. What color shirt will she be wearing, etc.

You can just ask yourself right now, please show me what YES feels like in my body. Ask yourself a question like is my name Harry? For me, lol it's a NO. Then I ask is my name Donna? So feel into the YES.

Begin practicing with questions that don't really matter as opposed to questions that are life altering decision when this is new to you. Such as…... Would I have a great time if I go to the Beach for the weekend? (Notice how it feels versus the next question.) Or would I enjoy staying locally more this weekend and going to that party? (Any change in how you felt from the first question?) Feel into your body and any subtle feelings especially in your stomach area. Or full body happy expansive feelings versus a sinking heavy feeling.

- A no or not the best option will feel hesitant and constrictive. Or tight maybe in your belly or heart or feel heavier or weighted. You may feel an ehhh…..not big excitement or not great.
- A yes may feel more free and open, expansive or lighter and really good. A feeling of more joy, mostly in my heart and upward feeling more of a yes or joy. Try it, how is it for you?

As you get comfortable with going into your body/mind/spirit, focusing on yourself to ask yourself how do I feel about this, you will begin to build that trust in what you are receiving. You can easily use this tool to check in when making bigger decisions when this is a regular practice. There will be times where you don't even ask. You just begin to notice how your body feels in any situation.

Messages outside of you!

To me THIS is where it gets incredibly fun. Asking for messages or signs, often after I pray about something and then I forget about it. Crazy coincidences happen, signs just seem to show up letting you know you are supported, on track or in flow. Sometimes it's just a hey we are here! You are so supported by this invisible realm of Heaven! (As I am proofing this paragraph and the garage door to my home literally just opened by itself, hello heaven!)

There was a time I didn't think I would ever understand messages or signs and I thought that my spiritual teacher had all the answers. How lucky was I that I had a teacher who showed me how to do this for myself? However, I learned from Spirit that Spirit speaks to each of us in our own language, in ways that are meaningful to each one of us. I didn't need to know every symbol or definition. They knew you before you knew you. What is meaningful to you is what will show, so don't be hard on yourself and dismiss things or assume you are wrong.

Value your own understanding and what is meaningful to you. How does it feel when you check within yourself around what you are questioning?

I am sharing a recent event for us, it was a day filled with signs that I thought would be a good example of how things can work. We had such a blast and great to know we had so much support. Most times it's really just "a" sign. Or a few. This particular day was loaded. I thought it would be fun to show you all of the ways you can see Spirit working with you throughout your day. In the places you may not think was anything and often go unnoticed.

She's gonna get it!

Jadin just recently took her driver's license exam. We had to drive out of town to York, Pennsylvania, otherwise we would have had to wait 6 more months. This was Jadin's second attempt. They were failing everyone that day of her first go round, she was told she went over the speed limit and didn't come to a full 3 second stop. (She has a different story, lol.)

We said our prayers this particular day, I sent energy ahead to our day and to Jadin and we hoped for the best. We were very early for her scheduled test and decided we could pass a little time to relax at a Starbucks for some coffee and a snack before we arrived to the DMV.

I searched for the closest Starbucks. It was located on *Donna Lane (my name)*. Our cashier's name was *Angelica*. (angel in her name.) The ladies room *smelled like my mom's favorite perfume.... Eternity* from Calvin Klein and the scent seemed to attach to me and I could still smell it as we sat waiting for our lattes. I asked Jay if she noticed the scent of my mom, she said yes she noticed. Then as I looked up at Jadin, I noticed right behind her was a *painting of many tea cups* as I was mentioning the Eternity perfume. My eye seemed to zoom in to particular design of a tea cup. I got up and walked over to the artwork to look closer at the writing underneath that seemed to draw me in, it said *Mimi*. Which Mimi some people use for *grandmother*. (My mom's perfume, and fancy tea cups remind me of my tea drinking Irish grandmothers and also my tea leaf reading great grandmother.) I pointed out all of our signs. I said to Jadin you are gonna do great!! AND your grandmother's are with you.

As we were driving to the test location, a car cut me off and was now right in front of me. The *license plate said "RUBY JAD."* So JAD first 3 letters of Jadin's name. One of the meanings of ruby is good fortune, and the Ruby slippers from the Wizard of Oz. "Dorothy you had the power all along" has meaning for me as we are so powerful! And lastly right next door to the DMV in York was in big yellow letters a store named *"Brimmer."* I stood staring saying, this is crazy! Never do I hear or see that name. It's my grandmother Criqui's maiden name in big bold letters. There was so much family support from the other side it was crazy! And *yellow is* the color related to the solar plexus, the power chakra. She had this!!

Jadin got the best examiner. Had a good experience, and of course she passed. So to review, a scent of my mom, Donna Lane, Angelica, a painting of tea cups symbolized my mom's mother and grandmother behind my daughter with the timing of talking about grandmother, the license and personal meaning with the first three letter of Jadin, and a my dad's mother's maiden name AND power color of yellow. It's not always lined with so many signs lol, so don't get disappointed. We prayed for lots of back up and I happened to be writing this section of the book. I am grateful for the heavenly support. Ask and it is given, right?

Coins or feathers

Sometimes angels or loved ones who have transitioned often appear to give you a thumbs up validating something you just did. Or maybe acknowledging the importance of something you just said. It could be them saying you are not alone and they are with you. Notice when you find your little treasure appearing as a coin or a feather, what were you thinking about, talking about or praying about. Most likely they are letting you know, it's going to be ok, or validating what you are thinking or saying. They are there with you, or you are loved and supported!

Coins

How do you figure out who is what coin? Why, you ask of course! Once I was told about this idea, I asked my guardian angel to please let me know how he/she would like to let me know when he or she was around? I kept finding dimes tail side up for days! In odd places, like literally jumped out of my shoe, in the clothes dryer, on the floor that I had walked past that same spot all day and there wasn't one minute, the next thing I knew it was there. Ok, dimes tail side up it is!

After my mom passed, I said ok mom how will you show to me mom? I really want to hear from you. I kept finding pennies. When my dad was passing, of course I was talking to my mom to be with us. I kept finding pennies at my feet everywhere. When Eric and I went to view a prospective new home the second time, for some reason I decided to look behind the walk-in closet door at the furthest corner almost magnetically, I don't even know on a conscious level why I did that. My eye went right to a penny. I showed Eric the penny, he knew what I was thinking.

Feathers

Ask the angels to send you a feather to let you know they are around. They may be letting you know they are helping you with a situation by leaving you a feather. Don't give up if it takes a while when you start this process. Keep asking and be patient. You can even ask the angels to make sure they point it out to you and it's in a clear path for you to know it's meant for you!

Often when I was doing hair at Bailiwick, I would have meaningful heartfelt conversations with my clients during our appointments. There were times more than I can count I would see a tiny white feather that seemed to drop out of nowhere from above me and dance dropping back and forth in front of my client and myself. I would point it out to my clients as it was playfully floating and dancing its way down. My eye seemed to be drawn right to it. It as if we were getting validations of …..we like this conversation, or what you are saying is true. I used to joke there must be a big pile of feathers up in the ceiling.

The day after my sister Patti passed I woke up to about a 4 inch long perfect beautiful golden yellow feather outside my bedroom door. It looked like it was placed there like a gift from St. Nick we used to get as kids outside of our bedroom door in the morning. Knowing this is so odd and questioning why would this be here, I totally felt this was a sign my sister passed through our home to visit us.

I do try to find a logical explanation if something unusual happens to see if there is an actual reason how something appeared. Because it's not out of the question one of my girls could have placed that pretty yellow feather outside my door because they thought I would like it. So I did ask them when I found the yellow feather, "hey where did you guys get this?" They replied with enthusiasm, "mommy that's pretty where did you get it?" No one knew where it came from.

Angel numbers

I have a beautiful friend through work who is in sales. My job as an educator sometimes is to have detail days with different sales people talking about my manufacturer's brand to salon owners. Of course we are in the car for HOURS together! My friend Jill-Ann is positive by nature and loaded with faith. We have had the best conversations on how she knows when she is receiving a message. She has asked the angels to help her with business and personal areas having faith, and regularly sees signs. When I met Jill-Ann she was single mom hoping to increase her income to make things a bit easier. She wanted to be successful and she works incredibly hard.

She kept seeing number combinations that relates to her dad which is 56. She often sees the letters JDF on license plates as she is out and about all the time. Her dad, mother, and brother all have the initials JDF (all of them have passed on.) Her eye is drawn to the clock at with the same number over and over everywhere she would point out when we were together. She sees all the time the number 333, 11 in many forms...711, 411. Her birthday is 4/11. She felt encouraged as everyday she would see the number patterns, seeing this helped her to keep the faith and knew better was coming.

Jill-Ann has risen to the top of the heap, she has earned a "can do" attitude by all those that know her, gotten a nice raise to help her cover an expanded territory, she was a top achiever with my brand at 163% of her goal and has gotten to go to Italy three times now with my company for her achievements.

Freddie my friend from North Carolina and I met at a training in Florida last year. We hit the ground running quickly as friends. I had done readings in Italy for about 7 women, he heard about it and asked me to chat. We chatted around how to keep positive movement forward regardless of setbacks. The importance of setting goals and to expect help among other tips of creating better in our lives. I shared that one action that propels us forward quickly is to free ourselves from our old ways energetically that are not serving us!

Before we got off the phone, something told me to mention to him the idea of angel numbers and to be on the lookout for number sequences. I gave him an example of years ago when I kept waking at 5:55 every day. It means big changes coming, you are safe during these changes. He said he doesn't get that kind of thing happening. I told him now that he knows about it to just observe what shows up. Well later that same day as I went to drive home from a class I saw Freddie tagged me in a post on facebook on my wall that stated 5:55. It happened later that same day his eye was taken to 555.

What's happening is the angels guide your eye seems to be drawn like a magnet somewhere - a clock, a license plate, a receipt number, number at the deli line, a telephone number. Once this becomes a form of your awareness, they now have a means for you to recognize them sending you a message in a way.

Soon after my mom passed I had a received a call from the phone number 000-000-0000 (expansion, endless, God, Oneness.) Where it usually says the town on the phone…it said, "out of the area" which I had never seen.

I answered my phone to hearing no one but it sounded like outer space. Lol, now this is how many crazy experiences I have had where my brain went when

I got this call. I listened for a few seconds and no one was there, just the outer space sound. I said…. MOM…..is this you? I almost expected her to literally hear her answer back. Or maybe you wake up at the same time throughout your week. Also start noticing the time someone calls you or texts you. Like 4:44. Or 1:11 Note the time stamp on the text or call, or posting.

Angel numbers sometimes depending on the source may slightly differ in their definition. Have no fear. The angels know what you are using as a resource. If you have a few like me, you see which resource and definition to which you are drawn. I have at one time kept Doreen Virtue's Angel Numbers book in my car or these days you can also get the app. You can get your answers quickly by using Pinterest or google to look up numerology or angel numbers.

I am going to provide a bit of generic for you to start with, but please look into what resonates for you in which could be in reading more into angels numbers, numerology or our Wish™ numbers in a book or article on pinterest or google. I recently learned about Joanne of Scribes for looking up angels numbers. So many great resources!

ANGEL NUMBERS

000- you are one with God, things have come full circle

111- pay attention to your thoughts, you are manifesting what you are thinking. A gateway is open. Be sure you think good thoughts!

222 - Keep going, new ideas are coming into fruition. Keep visualizing, affirmations, prayers and positive thoughts!

333- Ascended Masters shower you with love. Also Universal truth.

444- The angelic realm loves you and supports you.

555- Big changes are happening, shifts and transitions. You are safe in this process.

666- Harmony and balance. Bring your thoughts back to the present, spirit and service. When you do your emotional and material needs are met as a result of aligning.

777- You are in alignment with Universal flow. Expect more miracles. You are in a positive flow the angels applaud you!

888- A phase is about to end. The time is ripe, don't procrastinate enjoy the fruits of your labor.

999- Completion, A process, cycle or transition is concluding.

Before I learned angel numbers Nancy taught me what in a nutshell numbers in numerology meanings. Of course what I am giving to you now is a quick reference, you can study much deeper if it appeals to you!

I love "The Complete Idiot's Guide to Numerology Workbook" which I find to be on point and funny! You will learn how numbers have an energy vibration, how to calculate your life path number, destiny number, your name energetically. To me it's ironic what you learn and the correlation to who you are!

I know myself in my 20's I learned my life path was an 11, a master number. It seemed way too big for who I was at the time, at the very beginning of my spiritual enlightenment. 11's life purpose is showing others inspiration and enlightenment, healing, spiritual experiences, teaching others emotion and vibration create our reality. Pretty crazy right? That is exactly the where my path took me. Take a look at yours and see if you agree with your findings. It's fun to check out. Numbers have vibration!

Numerology

1- New Beginnings
2- Partnerships ~ can be a partnership here or your spiritual partnership
3- Trinity ~ The Holy Trinity or body/mind/spirit ~ creative vibe

4- Foundation - personal foundation or your home

5- Change

6- Family - your earthly family or spiritual

7- Spirit

8- Leadership - financial success - power

9- Completion, metamorphosis is taking place.

0- God, no beginning no end. Everything and nothing. Expansion and oneness. Adds to the energy of another number. Such as 10. New beginnings (something big)

You can even break down the numeric value and energy of an address, a name, etc. Each letter correlates with a number. You can add up the numbers and reduce the total. I realized my home when I was married was 400 Eagle Drive. I learned so much at this home that was different from my upbringing about my relationship with God. Creating a new foundation that resonated with the truth with in me. 4 is foundation 0 means expansion and/or oneness. Eagle can mean spirit. Which I learned so much about Spirit at my time in this home....the *foundation* of spirit at a much deeper level *expansion, oneness* with *God*. Exactly what I got in my time in that home. How about that?

Wish™ Numerology

When learning how to properly facilitate The Wish™, we were taught to observe what is being reflected not only in the game but also to have awareness around what is being reflected in our lives. The Wish™ numerology has become a way of life for me, and the numerology I feel resonates with me the most now. Remember Spirit speaks what is meaningful to you. To me it tells a story. I don't just break it down to a single digit like numerology, there is value reading the numbers as if it is a sentence if there is a number sequence.

I also expand on the message and may add the digits together and after I see and feel into the number story. There is a lot of sacred geometry in the Wish game and the numbers reflect sacred geometry teachings and also dimensional energy. I am not an expert in sacred geometry but boy do I know when numbers show up there is a message that is perfect.

There can be a few meanings associated with in each number. Check around which has significance for you in the moment. For instance I had a great conversation with Louise the creator of the Wish around plans with classes and opportunities coming up in the near future. I stopped on my way to work for coffee. In big numbers across the top was 343. (Life purpose) (Heart, universal compass) (Life purpose). The wish is all about energy - and being in your heart listening for divine direction, and certainly a part of my purpose. I was excited for the validation. Also 3+4+3=10. Break down the 10 to 1+0=1. 1 is about self, and to me in this instance oneness with God. Really the essence of this entire book. Self and God.

The Wish™ Numerology

1- Has to do with self. Your ego, identity. Can be separateness or "Oneness" with God.

2- Being in our heads, relating to others outside of you, relationship, intimacy

3- Being in our emotions, what's reflecting in our reality, life purpose, earth plane our choice

4- Being in the heart, career, financial freedom, direction - Universal compass

5- Personal power, Universal Energy, manifestation, synchronicity

6- Bliss, love, fun and adventure, happiness

7- Higher self - Spirit - Universal signs and guidance, spiritual order, truth, best answers

8- Universal opportunities, abundance, flow, infinity

9- Completion, perfection, matrix, portal

0- Expansion, opportunity

10- Quantum jump, ripple effect, complete freedom

11- Gateway or mirror being reflected to self

12- Self and relation to another or everyone

So look at my 400 Eagle Drive address from the Wish Numbers. The house number also reflects:

Heart, expansion, expansion

The heart is where we are one with God, where we receive our guidance. It's where you access the universal compass (listen for direction), your truth. Where your heart is the intersection of the earth plane and universal energy. Expansion to me means growing and expanding into Universal Truth, and being one with God. I learned so much about God, and hearing Heaven to create better at my time in that home. It is where I happened to delve deeper into understanding my spiritual path and hearing the Divine. Being in my heart, connecting to God and the angels I expanded to higher and better for me and my path.

For those of you interested, you can order your very own Wish™ game or learn more about the wish on our website. Thewish8.com

Sounds and smells

I asked spirit while sitting at a traffic light, is there anything else I should add in this section about signs? I heard smells. Then I saw a rose. I'm laughing because in my human mind I logically would think they'd would make a sound to me right? I find this with Spirit too. Things often come in different ways than I would expect. We never know how we will receive our answers! They always keep me on my toes and laughing.

Remember to use all of your senses to experience messages, including your actual hearing, vision, feeling, knowing, or sense of smell. I realized when I saw the rose in my mind's eye yesterday that my mom was the first to tell me about signs from above and the sign she received one time. It was through the sense of smell.....roses.

Roses in the fall

My grandmother had Parkinson's disease when I was very little. This was in the early 70's, and l'dopa was just coming out for treatment of Parkinson's and was experimental. My gram had been confined to a wheelchair and at this point was in a nursing home. Life had become difficult for gram, even communication was a challenge. My mom prayed to the Little Flower Saint Therese (the patron saint of her High School) that if her mom wouldn't improve with the new meds, that God take my gram. Please don't let her suffer anymore.

My gram actually passed away the following day. My mom and dad came back from saying their goodbyes at the nursing home and parked in our driveway when they returned home. It was a really cold day on November 1. My parents got out of the car and strongly smelled roses around the car in our driveway, the scent lingered for a quite bit of time. There were no flowers anywhere, all the leaves had fallen off of the trees, and there were no roses at our home. It was not the season, it was too cold. My mom told me roses were a sign of the Little Flower when a miracle occurs. She added that she knows my gram passing was an answer to her prayers.

So maybe you smell cigarettes for no reason, did someone you love who passed smoke? I have smelled for no reason in my home or car cigarette smoke. I have smelled incense like the smell of frankincense from mass in the Catholic church coming from inside my car. Or it has smelled like burning candles. I smelled fresh roses when none were there, fresh juicy oranges out of nowhere, my mom's perfume, men's cologne, cigars and woodsy scents all when it makes no sense to smell these things. I have as always tried to poke holes in the why, only to find there is no explanation. And other people validate that they smell what I am smelling too!

The most beautiful bell (hearing)

After my Angel Practitioner class with Charles Virtue I went to pick up my two daughters who stayed with my animal rescue friend Tara. I was so excited to share the exquisite high vibe experiences I had with my girls and Tara, how amazing the class was and how much I learned.

As we were speaking, all standing in a circle I heard this beautiful sweet peaceful bell pierce softly but strongly the space between us and then seemed to permeate the entire room downstairs where we stood. It was the "ting" of a bell and was the most beautiful angelic sounding bell and I could feel it ring through my body as well. I looked at Tara and said are you cooking something? Is that your timer? She looked me dead in the eye and said, I don't have a timer. I said did you hear that or was it just me?

Tara, Morgan and Jadin all said yes we heard it too. We just looked at each other like, well THAT was crazy! That was no doubt the angels and a very powerful experience that we all got to share!

Electricity and power

Have you ever noticed a power surge at a weird time? Like the lights blinking on and off, or a certain light? Or the TV shuts off by itself, or turns on by itself?

My entire neighborhood was devastated when our close friend and the most wonderful man Tom passed away in a car accident at 37 years old. As one family who were best friends of Tom's and his family approached the casket at the funeral home, the lights over the casket blinked on and off many times. Undeniably letting them know Tom was there.

During the eulogy at church his best friend was sharing stories and talking about good times he had with Tom. All of a sudden a loud obnoxious fire alarm went off. To the best of their efforts, the people in charge at the church had difficulty shutting off the fire alarm. The alarm kept on blaring for some time. The people who worked for the church were scurrying about the building and obviously concerned to disrespect the service. Tom's wife Michelle looked at us and smiled with bit of comfort. We all knew it was Tom.

Finally the alarm stopped, we all settled back returning to the eulogy. Only to have to start loudly blaring again. I think there were some people who wondered why are these people laughing at such a serious time, we were all so close to Tom that was so him! So funny, Tom wanting everyone to lighten up and let us know he was still around. So sounds and electrical glitches came as a gift to all of us that we are still connected. He made us feel so comforted and laughed at his antics.

My mom's prank

Bonnie who is a dear client of mine who is also Catholic gave me a special gift after my mom passed. She was having a mass dedicated to my mom on her birthday. I was getting ready to attend my mom's mass before work and I turned on the Today show as I always did. I was walking in and out between my bedroom and the bathroom. Last I heard was Matt Lauer on the set of the Today show reporting the news. The next thing instead I heard a priest singing parts of a mass and an organ playing on the TV. I thought, they are having mass on the Today show? This caught my attention.

I walked back into my bedroom and of course…..the Catholic Channel was now on my TV. No longer the Today show. I sat just watching in disbelief. How did that get on my TV? I looked at my remote which was face up, and nothing was bumping it. Because my explanation in that moment was well maybe something was laying on the remote and bumped it or it was upside down. NOPE! By itself with nothing around it, and face up.

My mom's mission in my adulthood was to get me to go to church regularly. It was a conversation often. I thought that was a hysterical way to acknowledge she was happy and aware I was going to church in her honor and her memory. You get the idea? It was meaningful to ME. No one else, but me. Mom let herself be known by changing the channel to the Catholic Channel. Lol. You could dismiss it as coincidence. Nancy taught me a long time ago, there are not coincidences!

CHAPTER 17

My Wish for You

My wish for you is to live your happiest life! To know that Heaven is available to help you in the most beautiful ways beyond what we think we understand. I hope if you didn't already know, understand that you are never alone. That there is great power and comfort in choosing not to do this walk of life alone. To look for God, the Universe in your everyday life and the know there is a language that the invisible realm of heaven is speaking to you in ways we are not often taught.

My wish is for you to remember to ask for Divine assistance or peace, no matter how trivial it may seem. And especially in those moments when life seems to overpower you. You are so very important, treasured and loved. Please remember your truth is YOUR truth. Your relationship with God may vary from someone else's. Don't be so hard on yourself and remember you are enough, you loved, and perfect in your imperfections. You are designed by Divine!

Remember when you practice being flow, being in awareness and authenticity you can turn up the love volume in your life and invite more greatness to you and your loved ones lives. You have the power to choose to be in alignment and trusting in life and the wisdom that is unfolding for you.

If it resonates with you consider the idea that we are all energy and a part of God's energy. Being aware that like attracts like in the Universe and the energy you are holding has an impact on what is showing up for you. You choose with your free will, your words, and your actions and where your minds dwells. All of your choosing and the energy you hold within you offer a vibration that invite in your experiences.

At the end of the day it serves you to surrender and trust in the Universal Wisdom. To allow this wisdom to guide your happenings and the unfolding. But do your part. Stay in peace and find your joy and gratitude each day. Sure you can create but remember to be detached from the end results of your wanting. Knowing you may receive better than you could ever imagine by allowing God's best.

I hope you have fun and are fulfilled recognizing everyday magic and miracles. Stay awake to the messages sent your way. And remember the value in being one and your relationship with the beautiful Creator of the Universe.

I feel there is no one way to God. I have thought about all the different teachings throughout the world for years. So many religions that exist, all seem to have a common denominator in recognizing a power greater than just ourselves. It may be different from another person's deity or how we address God in prayer. We all seem to ask for assistance at times and we are told to give thanks. We make offerings, for me growing up it was lighting a candle or giving up meat for lent or putting money in the collection. For some cultures and religions it could be offering fruit or incense, stopping to pray at certain times of the day. We all show and speak gratitude and we praise our God, whoever that is to each of us.

Many of us are taught to surrender in our religions and hand to our concerns over, value stillness and contemplation. Expressing love, gratitude and hope to our higher power and wait in faith and trust. Angels are common to many religions, there are sightings and miracles that happen all over the world. We are all invoking a power greater than our human selves. All of this is coming to the energy field of LOVE no matter the name, no matter the vision in our mind of who that entity is or looks like.

I feel whatever brings us to that state of peace and surrender has value for us. That peace and allowing puts us in a state of non-resistance. Whether it is through surrender, prayer, affirmations, the point is to get the feeling of allowing God and trust.

What I offered to you was just my truth, my experience. I am not trying to convert anyone. I hope to offer ways to deepen your relationship by knowing you can receive answers in ways maybe you didn't think are possible. I hear from people who I have helped who think I have some special power or gift. I don't. We ALL have this support, communication, opportunities and gifts from God. There was a time I didn't dream of half of the things I experienced along my opening to God in new ways.

From a little girl who felt misunderstood, who learned what was happening with the invisible realm was truly happening and that it was not her imagination. To a woman who throughout her life has had and keeps having a wild ride and profound experiences who wants to tell everyone you can do this, reach for love, be one with love. Love your neighbor, act with empathy and kindness as it affects the whole.

Relax, trust in the process and enjoy the unfolding. Pray and be one with God or whomever you honor. Knowing you have a key role in the grand scheme of things. And the biggest component with in this life is YOU. Remember to honor yourself, you are a creator and the Universe is listening.

Remember to put things in motion with just asking, allowing, and having faith in the best that will show and try not to judge the process, things are always in flow even if it appears things are standing still. T R U S T.

Thank you sincerely for spending time with me. I hope to hear someday the wonderful ways Heaven has helped you. And I would love to hear if somehow you learned to open to new ways that empowered you as a co-creator from reading about my experiences.

I hope to have expanded your understanding and possibilities in the language of spirit. May you be blessed, embrace and expand more LOVE (God) into your life. I wish for you to discover your true beauty, honor who you truly are and express your gorgeous self fully.

Blessings and love,

Donna xo

Just kidding, one more thing ~ My parting gift from Spirit ~

I happened to find this angel writing I did for myself as I was writing this book and starting to doubt myself. I asked God what would you like to tell me? I feel it is a great message that came through for everyone, not just for me. The end pertains to me and my self-doubts...but I feel the bulk of the wisdom in this writing is for everyone and worth sharing.

Understand when I receive a writing it comes quickly, sometimes moving so fast my human hand can not keep up and often is in a language that is not the way we speak. The () are me explaining the words that were dictated that don't always work with how we speak. So the () is me expanding on the essence and vibe I receive around it.

The journey of your soul is with Me.....

The Power of All is beside you, within you and without you

Surround yourself with Love, and hardship will fall away

Succumb to the power of your knowing and reach out with kind deeds

The world has forgotten it's not about them, it's about ALL

We learn, we grow by being together. We stretch, we find truth by living together. We inspire and sound by being together. (express our essence in word and vibration.)

Had we not been together, all would not exist. Discoveries of self, reflection, being, resting, exhausting the entire human experience lived fully is because of each other.

There is no one way to Me. Ego suggest difference, spirit suggests paths.

Your words have set me free in ways some will discover more. Your kind ways show people how to be child. You have taught for years, not just now. By being love, you created more love.

When you are sad, allow others to inspire you. And them to reflect your kindness back to you.

Deserving always, truth is knowing you are inspired from Me.

Clear thinking is inspired thinking. Spirit will free you when you are one with me.

Your time has not been wasted. Dreams cease when you stop. Continue toward your hope. I am here. Allow me to write in your book and I will see you through.

I would love for you to join me on Instagram and Facebook. You can also check out my website to discover ways I can help you or your organization and my contact information.

Instagram:
@donnacriqui

Facebook:
Donna Criqui – Author of Heaven Help Me

Website:
Trueinsightwithdonna.com

Printed and bound by PG in the USA